Scientific
blackjack
&
Complete Casino Guide

donald l. collver

ARC BOOKS
New York

ARC BOOKS are published by ARCO PUBLISHING COMPANY, Inc.
219 Park Avenue South, New York, N.Y. 10003

Portions of this book appeared in a higher-priced hardcover edition.

Library of Congress Catalog Card Number 71-137696

ISBN 0-668-02420-8

Printed in the United States of America

PREFACE

Blackjack or twenty-one is the only casino game that gives a player the opportunity to play at odds favorable to him. It is possible to do this through the application of the principles set forth in this book. Unlike other methods, this one depends primarily on logical thinking rather than on rote learning.

I developed it while dealing blackjack on the Las Vegas Strip. At first I was seeking for a way to help my dealing, not my playing. I was trying to form the habit of keeping track of the 10's and aces so that I would know when to reshuffle the cards against players who bet heavily toward the last part of the deck. My memory was too poor to keep a running count of the cards, so I worked out a way to keep track of the 10's as a proportion of the remainder of the deck without having to add up the cards. Before long I learned that, by using the same simple method, I could keep track of the small and medium cards as well.

The calculation of the percentages was the most time-consuming part of developing my system. It was necessary to make calculations for hundreds of situations. The results are presented in table form to show the action to be taken by the player in any given situation.

The self-tests presented throughout the book, as well as the training game, are designed to measure the skill acquired through the use of my principles of blackjack play. They are also, I might add, fun to do.

The second part of this book is an up-to-date casino guide. It gives the percentages for various casino games and information concerning house rules, size, location, and entertainment available in the foremost casinos in Nevada and other major gambling centers in the Western world.

I wish to thank Mr. Sil Petricciani, owner of the Palace Club in Reno, Nevada, for his help on various parts of the casino guide, and Mr. Stuart Schweizer, the Palace slot machine manager. Casinos which contributed to this book through photographs or casino information include the Sahara Tahoe Hotel, Hotel Tropicana, Caesar's Palace, the 4 Queens Hotel, the Riviera Hotel, the Kursaal d'Ostende, San Remo Casino Municipale, Casino de Monte Carlo, Casino Municipal de Cannes, International Spielbank-Lindau/Bodensee, Casino of Spa, Casino of Dinant, and the Condado Beach Hotel. I am indebted to my wife, Alicia, and to my brother, Bob, for writing assistance.

DONALD L. COLLVER

CONTENTS

6

PART ONE

SCIENTIFIC BLACKJACK WORKBOOK

1.

RULES OF BLACKJACK

THE FIRST CONCERN of a player who wants to master blackjack —or any game, for that matter—is a thorough understanding of the rules governing the play.

Since most players have probably played blackjack at home with friends, and "home rules" have applied, the player on his first visit to a gambling casino is usually somewhat bewildered by the casino rules. Confusion is heightened by the fact that these rules change and vary from casino to casino. It is important that the player review the rules—and in particular the rules of the casinos as listed in Chapter 19. It is always best, when in a casino, to consult the dealer regarding interpretation of house rules.

Layout

Blackjack is played on a semi-circular table covered with green felt. During the course of play, the dealer stands behind the table while the players sit opposite the dealer. There are usually spaces for six players, although some casinos use five and others seven spaces. On the table in front of each player is a circle, a square or other design on which the players place their wagers. All bets must be placed on or in this designated area before the start of each deal.

Sahara Tahoe Hotel-Casino, world's longest casino. Photo was taken from center of blackjack pit.

Cards

The cards used in blackjack are regular playing cards with fifty-two cards in the deck. Usually only one deck is used, although *double deck blackjack* utilizes two decks, and blackjack when played with a *shoe* may use several decks. The card value is as follows:

Ace—counted as either 1 or 11.
2 through 10—counted at face value.
Jack, queen, and king—counted as 10.

Deal

The cards are shuffled by the dealer and dealt to the players in turn, starting from the dealer's left to his right. The top card is either burnt (placed on the bottom of the deck, face up), or else a joker is placed on the bottom.

The dealer deals two cards to each player, including himself. The dealer's first card is turned face up and his second card face down under his *up* card. Usually, both of the players' cards are turned face down, but it does not really matter if the dealer sees a player's hand since he is required to play his cards in a set pattern regardless of any other hand. When playing double deck blackjack, the cards are all dealt face up, except the dealer's hand, which remains one up and one down.

Object

The object of blackjack is to get as close to 21 as possible without going over. If a player goes over 21, he automatically loses. If he is under 21 and the dealer is over, the player wins and the dealer loses. Going over 21 is called going *broke*. If the player and dealer both have the same count, it is called a *push* and neither wins or loses.

If the player receives 21 with two cards, he has a blackjack, and the dealer pays one and one-half times the amount bet. If the dealer has a blackjack, he will collect all bets before he hits the players. However, there are two exceptions when the dealer does not collect a bet: when a player takes insurance, which is explained later, and when a player also has a blackjack, in which case it is a *push*. When the player has a blackjack, he immediately turns his cards face up.

The player may stand or draw on any number. Drawing is called *hitting* and the player hits by *scratching* the table with the cards.

The player will always hit or take action on a hand less than 12, but it is sometimes wise to stand on 12 or over. A 12, 13, 14, 15, or 16 is called a *stiff*. The stiff plays the most important role in scientific blackjack since the frequency of the stiffs requires the player to make almost constant decisions concerning them.

After the player has all the cards he wishes, the correct procedure is to place the corner of the cards under the wager. If the player goes *broke*, his cards are turned face up. When all of the players are through hitting, the dealer then turns his hole card face up and hits his hand until he reaches 17 or over. In some casinos the dealer must hit on a *soft* 17 and in some casinos he must stand on it.

A soft 17 is an ace and 6, or any number of cards which add up to 7 with an ace as one of the cards. Any hand not counting an ace as 11 is called a *hard* hand. In Reno, Carson City, Lake Tahoe, and downtown Las Vegas, the dealer must hit a soft 17, whereas most Las Vegas Strip hotels have rules requiring the dealer to stand. The rules are usually written on the table. It is to the advantage of the player for the dealer to stand on a soft 17.

Doubling Down

Double down is the term used for doubling the wager and taking a hit card face down. A player should usually double on a 10 or an 11, although a soft 13 (ace and 2), and soft 14, soft 15, soft 16, soft 17, and a hard 9 are sometimes good double down bets. The correct occasions to double down will be explained in later chapters.

A player doubles down by turning his cards face up in front of his wager and doubles his wager before the dealer hits his hand. The wager does not have to be exactly doubled. If the player wishes, he may add any amount not to exceed the original wager.

Doubling

Splitting

The rules for doubling differ throughout the world—and often in casinos located side by side. Three of the ways casino rules differ are:

Player may double on any two cards.
Player may double on 10 or 11.
Player may double on 9, 10, or 11.

All casinos in Las Vegas and most North Lake Tahoe casinos will allow a player to double on any two cards. This means that he may double on a soft hand, such as an ace and a 4, but not on a hand having three cards such as a 2, 4, and a 5 hit card. In most Reno and South Lake Tahoe casinos the rules allow the player to double down only on 10 or 11. See Chapter 19 for the individual rules on doubling in various casinos.

Splitting

If the player has a pair (any two cards with the same value), the cards may be split and each may be hit separately. The player must put another wager, equal to the first, on the split pair.

For example, if the player bets $2 and receives a pair of 8's he may split them by placing an additional $2 in front of the second 8. The 8's are turned face up and the player plays each 8 as a new hand and hits each as many times as he wishes. If the player draws another 8, he may split the 8's again.

If the player splits aces, only one *hit* card is allowed each ace. If a split ace is hit with another ace, the house rules in most casinos will not permit the player to split aces a third time. When aces are split and a 10 is given either or both aces, the hand is not considered a blackjack, but simply a 21. Any two 10-value cards may be split, such as a king and a jack. After hitting a split card, some casinos will allow the player to double down, but most will not.

Insurance

In all Las Vegas casinos and most Reno and Lake Tahoe casinos, the player may take *insurance*.

Insurance means that when the dealer has an ace showing on his up card, the player may make an additional wager, betting that the dealer draws a blackjack. The amount of insurance that may be taken is any sum up to half the wager on the hand. The insurance wager is then paid double if the dealer has a black-jack; if not, the dealer takes the money.

The insurance wager is made immediately after the cards are dealt and is placed in front of the regular wager. When the dealer hits a blackjack, he will not take the regular wager or the insurance wager. If the player also has a blackjack, the dealer will pay the original wager once or the insurance wager double.

It is advantageous to make an insurance bet only if the dealer has a larger number of 10's in the remaining deck than is normal. This point is covered in the chapters on casing the deck.

Check Questions—Rules

1. If the player goes over 21, he loses unless the dealer goes over 21 also. .... T   F
2. If the player and dealer both have the same count between 17 and 21, they push and the bet is not lost. .. T   F
3. A soft 17 is a hand that has an ace, 6, and a 10. .... T   F
4. If the player doubles down, he may get only one hit card. .... T   F
5. If the player splits aces, he may get only one hit per ace; but if he splits any other pair, he gets as many hits as needed. .... T   F
6. Never take insurance unless you have two 10's. .... T   F

Answers: 1.-F; 2.-T; 3.-F; 4.-T; 5.-T; 6.-F.

2.

FALLACIES, SUPERSTITIONS, AND PSYCHOLOGY

MOST BLACKJACK players do not always think logically. They are prone to misconceptions which simply do not make sense and often they go in for rank superstitions. A beginning player runs the danger of acquiring some of these fallacies and absurdities the first time he plays. It would be wise to learn what they are before playing the game.

Hot and Cold Tables

The most widely held superstition in blackjack is the belief that there are hot and cold tables. This is so widely accepted that most pit bosses, dealers, and players are absolutely convinced that a table where players are winning is *hot* and a table where players are losing is *cold*. Usually players will raise their bets as a table gets *hot;* they may split 10's or double on bad hands in an effort to cash in on the hot table. When a player wins, he believes the superstition; when he loses, he considers himself a victim of phenomenal bad luck.

It is reasonable to say a dealer or a table has been running hot or cold in describing how the play has been going, but an intelligent player knows that a table which has been losing has an equally good chance to start winning—or vice-versa. Long winning streaks and long losing streaks are a matter of percentage—a cold mathematical fact which a player who wishes to win consistently must always keep in mind.

Table Hopper

The table hopper believes in a fallacy similar to the "hot and cold" tables. The illogical conclusion in this case comes from his experience in losing after sitting at one table for any length of time. And so he will move on from table to table after every few hands. This, of course, can in no way change the iron law of percentages.

Insurance

A major miscalculation in blackjack concerns the taking of insurance. Many players will take insurance when they have hands as good as 20 or blackjack. This is the very time when the player should not make an insurance bet because, by having two 10's in his hand or even one 10, he has reduced the dealer's chance of hitting a blackjack.

The logical way to decide whether or not to insure is to *case the deck*, which will be discussed later in the book. Another way is to look at as many up cards as possible. One out of every three cards showing should be a 10. If less than one out of three exposed cards are 10's, then take insurance.

Third Baseman

Another superstition subscribed to by blackjack players involves the *third baseman*. The third baseman is the last person to be hit. When he has a 12 or above hand and the dealer has a 6 or less showing, superstitious players believe the third baseman has helped a dealer hit a good hand if the third baseman hits.

Logically, it makes no difference which card the dealer takes. If the player is following the cards and knows the percentages, there are many times when he should hit the stiff.

Splitting 10's

Similar to the third baseman superstition is the ill-feeling against a player who splits 10's. Somehow they feel that the person who is splitting 10's is taking the dealer's break card or else a good card away from themselves. Needless to say, this is absurd.

Cutting the Cards

There are players who believe that it is hard luck to cut cards and so they refuse to do so. Probably the reason is that they remember losing after cutting and forget the times they won. No great problem arises if the cut is refused, but it does waste time.

Pit Bosses

Some pit bosses are also superstitious. They will change decks when the house is losing and leave them in when winning. Some bosses will change a dealer when he is losing. Like a baseball manager who will use his entire pitching staff to try to save a game, a pit boss sometimes runs through all his dealers.

Most players, especially those on a winning streak, resent changing the cards or the dealers. Professionals, however, take all this in stride. They know that the percentages remain constant.

Blackjack game in progress in Stateline, Nevada

PLAYING PSYCHOLOGY

Casino distractions can have a disastrous effect on players. The player who has trained himself to use the methods described in the following chapters must be able to keep his attention on the game. It is easy to let distraction interfere with playing concentration. Here are some of the distractions found in casinos and suggestions on how to eliminate them:

Distractions	Remedy
1. Dealer and players talking.	Try to be as inconspicuous and disinterested in chatting as possible. If you must talk, keep your eyes and mind on the cards at all times.
2. Free drinks offered.	Excessive drinking will obviously make concentration more difficult. Take orange juice or a soft drink while playing. Do your drinking when through playing for the evening, not at a blackjack table.
3. Friends and relatives.	If you must play near a friend or relative, try to avoid conversation while playing.
4. Entertainment in view.	It is just as easy to find a blackjack table away from the entertainment.
5. Fast dealers who are always rushing, have nervous habits, and have trouble counting, tend to upset serious player.	Try to keep your mind free from tensions. If you can't concentrate at one table, relax a few minutes and try a new table.
6. Toying with your money.	Even the best players often lose attention by counting their money or toying with it. Learn to leave the small mechanical distractions alone.

Perhaps it sounds boring to play without talking, drinking, looking about, or being with friends, but for many people it is the only way to keep their attention fixed on the game. This does not mean that everyone will be affected by the same distractions. It is up to the individual to know when he is not concentrating and to realize that it is important to pay complete attention to the game.

3.

SYSTEMS

BLACKJACK PLAYERS have been using systems as long as the game has been played. Most of these have been money systems of the progressive type, and the most successful has been a random progressive system based on the science of the game.

Straight Progression or Martingale ($1, $2, $4, $8, $16—)

This system is the double-or-nothing type of play that is common to almost all gambling. When the player loses, he doubles his wager, and when he wins he goes back to the original wager. For blackjack play, this is an unsuccessful system. The table limit is usually $500 or less, which means a $512 wager will be necessary on the tenth hand if one dollar is the first wager. It is not uncommon to lose as many as fifteen or more hands before winning.

Some players will reduce their chance of winning still further by not only doubling each bet when they lose, but by adding one dollar to the wager each time, so that when they do win they will actually win one dollar per hand. This method will reach a $511 wager on the ninth hand.

Numerical Progression ($1, $2, $3, $4, $5, $6—)

The numerical progression is not used often, but it is adaptable for blackjack play. The method adds one unit to the wager after each loss. This will not increase the wager nearly as fast as the Martingale and will fall short of reaching the table limit. It is unpopular because the player will lose overall if he doesn't win the first, second or third hand in each series.

Numerical progression can be thought of as a gamble between the player and the house as to whether the player will have winning and losing streaks of short or long duration. During a long period of play, winning or losing will still depend on how well the player plays.

Parlaying

This is directly opposite to those previously mentioned. The player allows his bet to ride while winning, and usually he has a pre-set number of times to let it stand before returning to the original wager. As a variation, the player will take a portion of his winnings and add it to the wager, continuing in this manner until he loses.

Parlaying reduces the player's chances of winning, because he will lose the larger wagers and win the smaller ones.

Cancellation System

The cancellation system is similar to the numerical system, and on the surface it seems unbeatable. It often draws attention because it requires the player to use paper and pencil in order to keep track of the betting.

The player usually writes down ten numbers at random, such as 3, 4, 2, 5, 1, 5, 4, 3, 1, 2. He then bets the total of the first and last numbers; if he wins, he crosses out the first and last numbers. In the above list of numbers the 3 and the 2 would be crossed out. If, on the other hand, he loses, he adds the lost wager to the end of the list, and the next bet will be the total of the newly added number and the first number on the list. Play continues in this manner until all the numbers are gone—or until the player reaches the table limit or goes broke.

When all of the numbers have been crossed off, the player will have won an amount equal to the original ten numbers. In our example, he would have won $30 if each number represented a dollar amount. If he reached the table limit before the numbers were all crossed out, he would have lost the total of all remaining numbers. On a $500 table limit, his losses might be several thousand dollars.

The player must win one out of three hands plus five hands out of approximately seventy to eighty hands played. The long range view of this system can be considered as a wager whereby the player must cross out all numbers from twenty to two hundred times for each time the limit is reached.

The following list illustrates a theoretical turn whereby the player will reach the casino limit before the numbers are crossed out. In this example he will lose two out of three hands until the limit is reached.

~~3~~				~~22~~	L			112	L		
~~4~~				~~27~~	L,	32	W	~~134~~	L,	156	W
~~7~~				~~26~~	L			138	L		
~~5~~				~~30~~	L,	34	W	~~164~~	L,	190	W
~~1~~				29	L			167	L		
~~8~~				~~32~~	L,	35	W	~~196~~	L,	225	W
~~4~~				~~30~~	L			197	L		
~~3~~				~~31~~	L,	32	W	~~221~~	L,	157	W
~~1~~				~~32~~	L			229	L		
~~2~~				~~34~~	L,	36	W	~~261~~	L,	293	W
~~5~~				~~31~~	L			266	L		
8	L,	11	W	~~42~~	L,	47	W	~~307~~	L,	344	W
~~9~~	L			46	L			312	L		
~~13~~	L,	17	W	~~55~~	L,	64	W	~~358~~	L,	404	W
~~11~~	L			57	L			367	L		
~~13~~	L,	15	W	~~68~~	L,	79	W	~~424~~	L,	481	W
~~16~~	L			73	L			424	L		
~~21~~	L,	26	W	~~89~~	L,	105	W	481	L		
~~17~~	L			90	L			Next Wager=$538			
~~18~~	L,	19	W	~~101~~	L,	124	W	over limit.			

Total Lost—48 hands = $5,852
Total Won—23 hands = $2,926
Net Loss $2,926

This illustration does not include doubling, splitting, black-jacks, or insurance, which could help or hurt the player. It shows that even though the original ten numbers were low, the system built up to large wagers quickly. It is not unusual to lose at an average rate of two out of three hands or win at a rate of two out of three hands. When the player wins at this rate, however, the winnings are only a small fraction of the loss.

4.

STRAIGHT PERCENTAGES

THE STRAIGHT Percentages Chart is the most important section of the book to learn. It describes the basic fundamentals of good play. Since blackjack is a game giving the player the option to hit, stand, split, or double down, the smart player will want to take the best action for each situation.

The chart covers all situations, assuming that the player is not casing the deck or that the count in casing the deck is even, as explained later. *Casing the deck* means to note mentally the denomination of the cards as they are dealt. Subsequent chapters will explain how to do this for blackjack play—a procedure which does not require unusual mental powers.

Some people bring charts and graphs to the blackjack tables to avoid memorizing the percentages. This is not an efficient method. It takes considerable time to look up a particular situation, thus distracting from casing the deck. The test questions at the end of the chapter will help you learn the percentage chart.

The straight percentage chart is calculated for the player playing in a casino where the rules require the dealer to hit a soft seventeen. There is little change in the play when the dealer must stand on a soft 17.

Interpreting the Chart

The Straight Percentage Chart is designed with three vertical columns representing the Player's Hand, the Dealer's Up Card, and the Action for the situation.

In using the chart, follow down the first column until you find your hand. The chart is read from left to right. The Dealer's Up Card is shown on the second column to the right of the Player's Hand. The correct action is in the third column, to the right of the Dealer's Up Card. When "all" is written in the Dealer's Up Card column, take the action shown at the right regardless of what card the dealer has showing.

STRAIGHT PERCENTAGES—DEALER HITS SOFT 17

Player's Hand	Dealer's Up Card	Action
8 or less	All	Hit
9	*6, 5, 4, 3, 2	Double
	Ace, 10, 9, 8, 7	Hit
10	10, 9, 8, 7, 6, 5, 4, 3, 2	Double
	Ace	Hit
11	All	Double
12	Ace, 10, 9, 8, 7, 3, 2	Hit
	6, 5, 4	Stand
13-15	Ace, 10, 9, 8, 7	Hit
	6, 5, 4, 3, 2	Stand
16	Ace, 9, 8, 7	Hit
	10, 6, 5, 4, 3, 2	Stand
17 or above	All	Stand
Ace, Ace	All	Split
2,2 and 3,3	7, 6, 5, 4, 3, 2	Split
	Ace, 10, 9, 8	Hit
4,4	All	Hit
5,5	10, 9, 8, 7, 6, 5, 4, 3, 2	Double
	Ace	Hit
6,6	6, 5, 4, 3	Split
	Ace, 10, 9, 8, 7, 2	Hit
7,7	7, 6, 5, 4, 3, 2	Split
	Ace, 10, 9, 8	Hit
8,8	All	Split
9,9	9, 8, 6, 5, 4, 3, 2	Split
	Ace, 10, 7	Stand
10,10	All	Stand
Ace, 2-5	Ace, 10, 9, 8, 7, 4, 3, 2	Hit
	*6, 5	Double
Ace, 6	Ace, 10, 9, 8, 7, 2	Hit
	*6, 5, 4, 3	Double
Ace, 7	8, 7, 3, 2, Ace	Stand
	10, 9	Hit
	**6, 5, 4	Double
Ace, 8-10	All	Stand

*If doubling is not allowed, hit.
**If doubling is not allowed, stand.

To illustrate, let us suppose you have a 14-point total and the Dealer's Up Card is 7. Follow down the column under Player's Hand until you see 13—15. This indicates that you should take the same action against the dealer's card whether your total is 13, 14, or 15. Follow the line across to the Dealer's Up Card. The 7 is on the first line directly to the right of the Player's Hand. Continue to the right and you will see the word "Hit." This indicates that you should hit his hand.

Suppose you have a pair of 7's and the dealer has a 9 up card. Follow the Player's Hand column to "7, 7," then follow the line to the right and find the "9" on the second line down. Continue to the right to the word "Hit." The player should hit rather than split or stand.

Use of the check questions

The check questions for this chapter and the following chapters are every bit as important as the text. Unless they are learned thoroughly, you cannot expect to remember the basics of good play when in a casino.

It is best not to write the answers in the book as you will want to repeat the questions many times. The most effective way to test yourself is to go through the questions one at a time and think out the answer. If you are certain you know the general rule for the situation, then go on to the next question. If you are not certain of the general rule, refer back to the chart and find the correct answer. By *general rule* is meant all the actions possible for any given hand you might hold. The general rule for a 16 hand would be: Hit when the dealer has an ace, 9, 8, or 7 up card and stand when the dealer's up card is 10, 6, 5, 4, 3, or 2.

Do not attempt to study the following chapters on blackjack until you have answered the questions in this chapter several times and have mastered the general rules. The chart is the foundation upon which succeeding charts will be based.

Questions 31 through 43 should always be reviewed the day before playing in a casino, even when you are playing regularly. If you miss on some of the questions, review the general rules until the questions can be answered with ease.

CHECK QUESTIONS—STRAIGHT PERCENTAGES

(What action should be taken for the following situations?)

1. Player has 3 & 4—dealer has a 6 showing   . . . . . .
2. Player has 4 & 5—dealer has a 2 showing   . . . . . .
3. Player has 3 & 8—dealer has a jack showing   . . . . . .
4. Player has 5 & 7—dealer has a 4 showing   . . . . . .
5. Player has 9 & 7—dealer has a 7 showing   . . . . . .
6. Player has 8 & 9—dealer has a king showing   . . . . . .
7. Player has 2 & 2—dealer has a 7 showing   . . . . . .
8. Player has 5 & 5—dealer has a 9 showing   . . . . . .
9. Player has 9 & 9—dealer has a 2 showing   . . . . . .
10. Player has ace & 4—dealer has a 4 showing   . . . . . .
11. Player has ace & 7—dealer has a 4 showing   . . . . . .
12. Player has 2 & 7—dealer has an 8 showing   . . . . . .
13. Player has 6 & 6—dealer has a 3 showing   . . . . . .
14. Player has 6 & 7—dealer has a 2 showing   . . . . . .
15. Player has 3 & 3—dealer has a 10 showing   . . . . . .
16. Player has 4 & 4—dealer has a 6 showing   . . . . . .
17. Player has ace & 6—dealer has a 7 showing   . . . . . .
18. Player has 7 & 7—dealer has a 7 showing   . . . . . .
19. Player has ace & 5—dealer has a 5 showing   . . . . . .
20. Player has ace & 8—dealer has a 6 showing   . . . . . .
21. Player has ace & 7—dealer has an 8 showing   . . . . . .
22. Player has 7 & 7—dealer has an 8 showing   . . . . . .
23. Player has ace & 7—dealer has a 3 showing   . . . . . .
24. Player has 6 & 6—dealer has a 7 showing   . . . . . .
25. Player has 9 & 9—dealer has a 9 showing   . . . . . .
26. Player has 7 & 7—dealer has a 5 showing   . . . . . .
27. Player has 3 & 7—dealer has an ace showing   . . . . . .
28. Player has 4 & 10—dealer has a 2 showing   . . . . . .
29. Player has ace & ace—dealer has an ace showing   . . . . . .
30. Player has 2 & 2—dealer has an 8 showing   . . . . . .

On questions 31 to 43, give the correct action for all values of the dealer's up card.

31. When the player has 11 . . . . . .
32. When the player has a pair of 2's or 3's . . . . . .
33. When the player has a soft 17 (ace and 6) . . . . . .
34. When the player has 13, 14, or 15 . . . . . .
35. When the player has a pair of 9's . . . . . .
36. When the player has 9 . . . . . .
37. When the player has 16 . . . . . .
38. When the player has ace and 7 . . . . . .
39. When the player has a pair of 6's . . . . . .
40. When the player has 12 . . . . . .
41. When the player has a soft 12 to soft 15 . . . . . .
42. When the player has a pair of 7's . . . . . .
43. When the player has a pair of 4's or aces . . . . . .

5.

BEGINNING CASING

THE STRAIGHT Percentage Chart in the preceding chapter is the basis of smart play. However, as the cards are dealt and discarded, the proportion of 10's to the rest of the deck is constantly changing, as is the proportion of 9's and 8's and so on. This fact can be used to advantage by adjusting the straight percentages to compensate for the changes as they occur.

There are two difficulties in keeping track of the changes. First, a method must be learned and, second, the adjustment to be made on the Straight Percentage Chart must also be learned. An easy way to keep track of the changes in proportion will be presented in this chapter. Although *casing the deck* will be the designation for keeping track of the proportion of the deck, this will not be like keeping track of all the cards, as will be shown.

The technique for casing presented in this chapter takes most of the memorizing out of the standard methods. It substitutes a mechanical system which is devised to give the desired information in a form which clearly and directly spells out the changes in the deck.

Before learning the mechanics, it is necessary to understand the reasons for casing in the manner presented. To illustrate these reasons, the deck must be analyzed. There are sixteen cards with a 10-denomination, four cards each of 9, 8, 7, 6, 5, 4, 3, 2, and ace denominations. If each card were cased by itself, you would have to keep track of the total number of cards as well as a total for each denomination, and then divide the totals to find the percentage. Obviously, it would be impossible to do this for each denomination and then analyze all the individual percentages to find the effect of the change in proportion of the deck Consequently, this procedure must be simplified to a more practical form.

In analyzing the deck, the denominations can be separated into three sections of equal size, with aces counted separately. This division puts all 10's in one group, 9, 8, 7, and 6 in another group, 5, 4, 3, and 2 in the third group. Each group includes sixteen cards. The high, medium and small groupings have much more practical value in analyzing a particular situation than each denomination does individually. It can be seen that if you know that there are a greater proportion of small cards in the deck than normal —and you have a 15 or 16—your chances for making a good hand are improved. The medium group is beneficial for the small stiffs (12 and 13), and the 10's are beneficial for the double down plays, insurance, and knowing the chances for breaking.

Casing the Deck

The complete method for casing 10's, medium cards, and small cards will be presented in Chapter 7. Before learning how to case all three groups, the chapter on beginning casing will present only a portion of the technique in order to allow you to learn and train yourself on the basic fundamentals of the method. The 10's group will be the only cards cased. Knowing the proportion of 10's to the rest of the deck will give you a decided advantage, and for some players this may be as far as they wish to go in Scientific Blackjack.

The crux of this method is in realizing that one-third of the deck, minus the aces, are 10's. If the cards are observed in groups of three, then one out of every three cards should be a 10. Instead of counting the 10's as they are played, the player should keep a running proportion in the following way:

If there are no 10's showing out of three cards dealt, the count is one plus—the one plus meaning one extra 10 left in the deck in proportion to the remainder of the deck. If there are two 10's in the next group of three, the count is one minus—the one minus meaning one less 10 remaining in proportion to the rest of the deck. As each group of three cards is turned up, a running count is kept. Aces are counted separately and are not included in the sets of three.

Follow the sets of three in the illustration below and keep count as shown in parenthesis:

3, jack, 5 (even)	Ace, K, 7, 4 (2 aces and even)
9, 2, 7 (1 plus)	4, 2, 5 (1 plus)
8, 5, 6 (2 plus)	3, 7, 2 (2 plus)
K, 10, Q (even)	4, Q, 6 (2 plus)
8, ace, Q, K (1 ace and 1 minus)	8, 7, K (2 plus)
2, 9, 6 (even)	9, 3, ace, J (3 aces and 2 plus)

In the first group of three cards, there was one 10, the jack, so the count is even. In the next group of three cards, there were no 10's, so a one plus indicates an overbalance of 10's in the deck. The next group is also without a 10, so the overbalance of 10 is increased to two plus. The next group has three 10's, so the two extra 10's out of the three cards take away the two plus, and the count is back at even. In the next group, the ace is counted separately and the extra 10 out of the three cards, not counting the ace, leaves an underbalance of 10's, indicated by the one minus.

In the next illustration, the count will be omitted for most of the groupings. Always say the count to yourself for each grouping. This is necessary if the count is to be kept accurately.

J, 10, Ace, 5	6, 9, 6
J, 8, 6	6, 4, 2
3, 8, 3	9, 3, 7 (2 plus)
Q, 2, J (1 minus)	Q, 3, 10
Ace, 8, Ace, 9, 7	K, 2, 5
Q, 7, 4	10, 2, 9; 4, K, K;
10, 5, K	5, Q, 8 (even)
J, Ace, 7, 4	

In order to keep count rapidly, some practice is necessary. Take a deck of cards and turn the cards over one at a time and keep count. The count should end up at four aces and even. After going through the deck a half dozen times rapidly and accurately, have someone act as a dealer and practice casing the 10's and aces while playing. Start with one hand, then two, three, four, five, and six hands.

In order to gain the full benefit from casing, try to keep track of the cards as soon as they are exposed. The first three cards will be the dealer's up card and your own hand. Then as the dealer hits the players, keep count of every three hits. The next cards will be the dealer's hole card and hits. Then each player's hand is opened and picked up by the dealer. When the dealer has dealt all the cards from the deck, he shuffles the discards and continues dealing. Sometimes he will have dealt all the cards before the hand has been completed; at other times, after the hand has been dealt.

When the dealer has dealt out all the cards, erase the count to zero aces, and even 10's. Then recase all exposed cards.

This is the most difficult part in casing cards. Keep alert and when the dealer shuffles, always say, "Zero aces and even 10's," otherwise the change is easily missed. After you have become sufficiently skilled at casing the 10's, the method of reversing the count at the end of the deck, as described in Advanced Casing, should be mastered.

With just a little practice, casing 10's and aces can easily be learned. If a person has the desire to win, he should have the patience to learn the necessary skills. Unfortunately, casinos are noisy and offer many distractions. A player who wishes to case cards must discipline himself against these distractions. Excessive drinking, talking to players, watching entertainment, and counting money are some of the distractions to be overcome.

Weight of the Count

In the next chapter the charts show how the 10's affect the straight percentages. These charts are made with the understanding that half the deck has been cased. This is important to bear in mind, as shown in the following examples.

Suppose the count is one plus after only three cards have been cased. The case represents an overbalance of $2\frac{1}{6}$ percent of the deck, not including the aces. If the count is one plus after all but three cards have been cased, the overbalance is $33\frac{1}{3}$ percent. With half the deck having been cased, the overbalance is $4\frac{1}{6}$ percent. Consequently, the count must be adjusted to represent the correct *weight* of importance when using the charts.

The following table shows how much weight should be given to the count when various number of cards have been cased:

WEIGHT TABLE

Number of Cased Cards (Less Aces)	Proportion of Deck Cased	Multiply Count By
0	0	1/2
12	¼	2/3
24	½	1
32 (16 left)	⅔	3/2
36 (12 left)	¾	2
42 (6 left)	⅞	4

A method is now needed for determining the number of cards cased so that the weight table can be used. The most accurate —but least practical—method would be to count the cards as they are cased. Obviously, this would take a high degree of concentration and is difficult to perform.

The most common and most practical method for determining the number of cards cased is visual. The dealer will normally place the cards, as they have been played, under the deck in a face-up position. A distinct separation of the new cards and discards can usually be seen from the side view to the deck. When the dealer uses a tray for the discards, there is little doubt as to the proportion of cards cased.

Another way to find the amount of cards used is by approximating or counting the number of sets of three cards you have cased. If four sets of three have been cased, then one-fourth of the deck has been cased. This method is very accurate for the first part of the deck, but not for the last part, unless the sets of three are counted.

You will not need to determine the weight of the count for each hand. The only time it is needed is on the close plays. As a practical matter, an approximation of the proportion that has been cased is as accurate as is needed.

If you can see that the dealer has about half the deck discarded, then the weight of the count shows a multiplier of one. This means that if the count is two plus, it is multiplied by one, leaving the count two plus. If about two-thirds of the deck has been cased, then the count is multiplied by three-halves or one and one-half. A two plus would equal three plus in this situation.

As you get used to adjusting the count by the weight table, it should not take long before you automatically think of the proportion as the multiplier. For example, when you see that you have cased three-fourths of the deck, you automatically think in terms of multiplying the count by two.

To further illustrate the weight table, suppose the count is one ace and three plus in 10's with approximately twelve cards having been cased. A situation comes up to hit the hand if there is a three plus in 10's, but to stand if there is a two plus or less. From the table, the weight of the count is two-thirds of the three plus, which equals two. Therefore, the action should be to stand.

As another example, suppose a situation comes up calling for a stand action unless the count is two minus or more on the minus side. The count is one minus with about ten cards left uncased. What is the action? From the table you find that the weight is over two times the count; therefore, the one minus count should be considered as two minus or greater. The correct play would be hit.

CHECK QUESTIONS—CASING THE DECK

1. Case the following groups of cards:
   8, 9, 8   4, 2, 9   K, 10, 5   K, J, 4   A, 7, 7, 9   Q, 3, 6
   3, 5, 8   3, 2, 10.
   What is the count?
   Answer: One Ace and two plus.

2. Case the following:
   4, Q, 5   10, K, K   3, K, 5   J, A, 6, 7   6, 4, J   3, 4, 9
   10, K, 8   Q, 2, 6, A   5, 10, J   2, 3, Q.
   What is the count?
   Answer: Two Aces and three minus.

3. Case the following:
   2, K, A, 6   8, K, 3   A, 7, 2, 5   4, A, 10, 9   7, 7, 10
   9, 8, K   6, 9, 8   4, J, 9   5, Q, 3   Q, J, 4   5, 6, Q
   10, 5, 2.
   What is the count?
   Answer: Three Aces and one plus.

4. Case the following:
   5, 9, 3   7, K, 10   6, 3, 2   2, 8, 4   10, Q, 7   9, 8, 8
   5, 5, K   K, J, 7   A, 4, 3, 3   J, A, 2, 7   9, 6, A, 10
   Q, J, 10   Q, K, 4   4, Q, 6   8, J, 2   6, 5, A, 9.
   What is the count?
   Answer: Full deck, count should be four aces, even.

5. Case the following:
   8, 5, 7   9, J, A, K   K, Q, 10   6, 10, 4   5, 8, Q   5, 3, 9
   7, 4, 10   9, J, K   J, A, A, 6, 7   8, Q, 10   J, 3, 3   2, 3, Q
   A, 5, 9, 6   K, 2, 8   2, 4, 4   2, 7, 6.
   What is the count?
   Answer: Full deck, count should be four aces, even.

6. Case the following:
   2, 8, 3   5, 2, 7   9, 2, 6   A, 5, Q, 4   5, 8, 10   4, 3, Q
   K, 3, 6   7, 2, 9   A, J, 5, 9   7, 6, A, J   10, 8, J   Q, 10, K
   10, J, 8   7, A, K, 3   9, K, 6   4, Q, 4.
   What is the count?
   Answer: Full deck, count should be four aces, even.

7. The dealer shuffles a full deck and deals the player a Q and 3, and himself a 3 face up. He then hits a player with a 10, which breaks the player's hand of K and 5. What is the count?
   Answer: Zero and one minus.

8. The count is four aces and one minus in 10's; the dealer has a 7 showing and you have a 10 and 2. The third baseman has been hit with a 3 and a 9; the next player was hit with a 5. The dealer runs out of cards and shuffles. What is the count?
   Answer: Zero and one plus (always start back at "zero and even").

9. The count is four and one plus with the dealer having a Q face up and the player has a 3 and 5. The dealer runs out of cards and shuffles. He then hits the first player with a 10 and the next player with a 3 and a K. What is the count?
   Answer: Zero and minus one.

10. If about half the deck has been seen and cased, how much weight does the count contain?
    Answer: Full weight.

11. If about two-thirds of the deck has been seen and cased, how much weight does the count contain?
    Answer: Three-halves or one-and-one-half times the count.

12. If six cards are left and the count is three and two plus, what is the adjusted count?
    Answer: Three and eight plus. (Four out of the six remaining cards are 10's. Out of these six cards, one will be the "burnt" card and one will be the last card.)

13. If about six or seven cards are left, what is the weight of the count?
    Answer: Four times the normal weight.

14. If only eight cards have been seen, and the count is one and two minus, what is the adjusted count?
    Answer: Approximately one and one minus.

15. If three-fourths of the deck has been cased, and the count is one ace and one minus, what is the adjusted weight?
    Answer: One ace and two minus.

6.

BEGINNING VARIATIONS

CASING THE 10's will do little good if you don't use the case to your advantage. This chapter presents tables and graphs to illustrate the application of casing.

To attain the most benefit from the tables, you should learn how to analyze any basic situation that may arise. The correct play can be determined by associating the case with the particular situation. You will be able to rely on logic rather than on memory by learning the variations on the straight percentages.

Insurance

The information gained by casing the 10's can be utilized most directly through taking insurance. When the dealer has an ace showing on his up card, most casino rules permit the player to bet that the dealer has a 10 under the ace. This is called insurance because it can be considered protection for the original wager of the hand. If the dealer has a blackjack, then the insurance wager is paid two to one, although the original bet is, of course, lost. Needless to say, the smart player places the insurance wager only when the odds are in his favor.

Mathematically, the odds for receiving a 10 should be one out of three cards in order to play insurance at zero house advantage. If the aces are taken out of a full deck, one out of three cards should be a 10. Since the aces are not removed, they must be overcome by a plus count in 10's to swing the advantage to the player.

When the only ace that has been cased is the ace up card, the player should have a two plus in 10's to obtain a favorable advantage for insurance (a one plus in 10's is even odds). When more than one ace has been cased, a one plus in 10's is a favorable advantage. The weight of the case has no affect on the count for insurance.

Stiffs

Since the problem that arises most often in playing blackjack is trying to decide when to hit a stiff and when to stand, the stiff will be given special emphasis.

The stiffs for the straight percentages are illustrated in Graphs 1A and 1B. These graphs are not presented for memorizations, but they should be studied in order to understand the percentages that must be overcome to change the action.

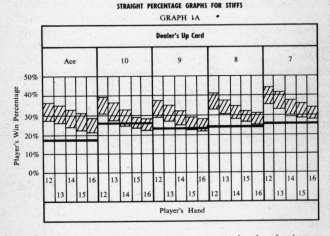

STRAIGHT PERCENTAGE GRAPHS FOR STIFFS

GRAPH 1A

NOTE: The heavy line in each column represents the player's win percentage if he stands. The bottom of the cross section represents the player's win percentage if he hits, and the remainder of the cross section is a push.

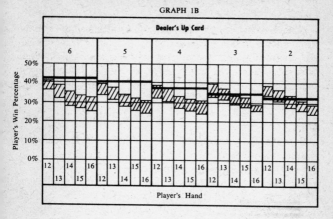

GRAPH 1B

The top line of each graph shows the dealer's up card, and the bottom line of each graph shows the player's hand. The cross sections represent the push area; the bottom of the push area is the player's win percentage. The heavy line through each section of the graph is the dealer's *break* line. This line represents the player's percentage of winning, should he stand. If the break line is at a higher percentage than the center of the push area, then the action is to stand. If the center of the push area is higher than the break line, then the action is to hit.

The relationship between the break line and the push area will give a clue as to how much overbalance of 10's, small cards, or medium cards is needed to change the action. When, for example, the player has a 13 and the dealer has a 2 or a 3, there is almost no difference between the break line and the push area. Since the situation is very close, the action can be expected to depend upon an overbalance of 10's or medium cards. If 10's are cased, a plus count in 10's will lower the percentage for hitting and raise the break line. A distinct separation of the area, favoring a stand action, will be evident. A case of minus 10's will raise the push area and lower the break line, showing a hit action.

The Stiff Table shows the case needed for changing the action of the straight percentage chart. An example of the use of this table is as follows:

STIFF TABLE (Player Cases 10's)							
Player	Dealer	Case	Action	Player	Dealer	Case	Action
12	2	1+	Stand	12	6	1—	Hit
13	2	1—	Hit	13	6	1—	Hit
14	2	2—	Hit	14	6	3—	Hit
15	2	2—	Hit	15	6	4—	Hit
16	2	3—	Hit	16	6	5—	Hit
12	3	1+	Stand	12-16	7	any	Hit
13	3	1—	Hit	12-16	8	any	Hit
14	3	2—	Hit	12-14	9	any	Hit
15	3	3—	Hit	15	9	3+	Stand
16	3	3—	Hit	16	9	3+	Stand
12	4	1—	Hit	12	10	4+	Stand
13	4	1—	Hit	13	10	4+	Stand
14	4	2—	Hit	14	10	2+	Stand
15	4	3—	Hit	15	10	2+	Stand
16	4	4—	Hit	16	10	1—	Hit
12	5	1—	Hit	12	ace	5+	Stand
13	5	2—	Hit	13	ace	4+	Stand
14	5	3—	Hit	14	ace	4+	Stand
15	5	4—	Hit	15	ace	3+	Stand
16	5	5—	Hit	16	ace	3+	Stand

DIRECTIONS FOR READING THE TABLE

1. Read down from Player for the player's hand and down from Dealer for the dealer's up card.
2. The case is given in plus or minus tens.
3. The Action column gives the reverse of the straight percentage chart. As long as the case is equal to the case listed or greater, the straight percentage action will be reversed.

NOTE: The case represents the count when one-half of the deck has been cased.

The player has 15 and the dealer has a 2 up card. The straight percentage chart indicates standing. If the case is two minus in 10's, the stiff table indicates that the player should change the action to hit. The weight of the count should be considered in order to determine the actual case. Referring back to the weight table, we see that if the count had been one minus in 10's with only ten or twelve cards left uncased, then the case would be equal to two minus in 10's and the player should hit.

The best way to study the stiff table is by grouping similar types of stiffs together. The most important grouping to remember is the 12 and 13 stiff against the dealer's stiff up card. (Stiff up card is a 2, 3, 4, 5, or 6.) As shown by graph 1A, the percentages to hit or stand are very close. A general rule for all of these situations would indicate hitting, if the case is one or more minus and standing on an even or plus case.

There are two exceptions to this rule. A 12 stiff, when the dealer has a 2 or 3 up card, should be hit if there is an even or minus case, and should stand if there is plus case. The second exception is when the player has 13 and the dealer has a 5 up card. This situation takes a two or more minus in 10's to hit.

The next grouping is for the 14 stiffs. Against the dealer's 2, 3, or 4 up card, a two or more minus case is needed to hit. Against the dealer's 5 or 6 up card, a three or more minus case is required to hit.

The 15 and 16 stiff hands against the dealer's stiff up card should be studied as a group. This group is not as important as the smaller stiffs since it takes a much larger overbalance of 10's to indicate hitting. As the dealer's up card progresses from a 2 to a 6, the case must progress from a two minus to a four minus for the 15 stiff, and from a three minus to a five minus for the 16 stiff.

For example, the player has a 15 and the dealer has a 4 up card. The player, recalling the two to four minus rule, would hit only if the case was three or more minus.

A stiff hand against the dealer's 7 or 8 up card should always be hit. When the case shows a plus count in 10's, the dealer has a good chance of hitting 17 or 18, and a good chance to win or tie with a 17, 18, 19, 20, or 21. When the count is minus in 10's, the dealer is less likely to have a 17 or 18. With the addition of small cards, however, both the player and the dealer has a good chance to hit without breaking.

Against a 9 up card, the player should hit all 12, 13, or 14 stiffs. The 15 and 16 stiffs should be hit except when the case is three or more plus.

When the dealer has a 10 up card and the case is plus in 10's, the player's chances to win after hitting are diminished. Likewise, the dealer has a good chance to make 20 or a good chance to break, if he has a stiff hole card. By reasoning in this manner, the player should recall the action. If the player has a 16, he should stand against a 10 up card unless the case is one or more minus 10's. If the player has a 15 or 14, he should hit unless the case is two or more plus. He should stand on a 13 or 12 only if the case is four or more plus.

When the dealer has an ace up card, the player should hit all 16 or 15 stiffs unless the 10's count shows three or more plus. For the 14 or 13 stiffs, the case must be four or more plus, and for a 12 stiff the case must be five plus.

The check questions at the end of this chapter provide training for learning the stiff table. The questions should be answered as many times as needed to master the contents of the table.

Double Down

Casing 10's is advantageous for the *double down* situations, as the 10's will directly affect an 8, 9, 10, 11, soft 17, soft 18 soft 19, or soft 20. It should be noticed in the Doubling Table that only a small overbalance of 10's will affect these situations.

Do not underestimate the importance of the double down. The player who does not take advantage of doubling will lose his best payoff hands. A wrong decision in doubling will cost twice as much as one made on a stiff hand.

Unlike the stiff table, the doubling table has no large groupings to show generalizations. The check questions are the best means of learning this table. Here are two examples illustrating the use of this table.

> *Example 1:* The player has an 11 and the dealer has a 9 up card. The
> player will double unless the case is one or more minus in tens.
> *Example 2:* The player has 9 and the dealer has an 8 up card. The
> player will hit unless the case is one or more plus.

				DOUBLING TABLE (Player Cases 10's)			
Player	Dealer	Case	Action	Player	Dealer	Case	Action
11	ace	1–	Hit	8	6	1+	Double
	10	1–	Hit		5	2+	Double
	9	1–	Hit		4	2+	Double
	8	2–	Hit		3	3+	Double
	7	3–	Hit		2	3+	Double
	6	any	Double	Soft 13	6	1–	Hit
	5	any	Double	Soft 14	5	1–	Hit
	4	any	Double	Soft 15	4	1+	Double
	3	4–	Hit	Soft 16	3	3+	Double
	2	3–	Hit		2	3+	Double
10	ace	1+	Double	Soft 17	6	3–	Hit
	10	1–	Hit		5	3–	Hit
	9	1–	Hit		4	2–	Hit
	8	2–	Hit		3	1–	Hit
	7	3–	Hit		2	1+	Double
	6	any	Double	Soft 18	6	3–	Stand
	5	any	Double		5	3–	Stand
	4	any	Double		4	2–	Stand
	3	4–	Hit		3	2+	Double
	2	3–	Hit		2	2+	Double
9	ace	any	Hit	Soft 19	6	2+	Double
	10	any	Hit		5	2+	Double
	9	any	Hit		4	2+	Double
	8	2+	Double		3	2+	Double
	7	1+	Double		2	3+	Double
	6	3–	Hit	Soft 20	6	2+	Double
	5	2–	Hit		5	2+	Double
	4	1–	Hit		4	2+	Double
	3	1–	Hit		3	2+	Double
	2	1–	Hit		2	3+	Double

DIRECTIONS FOR READING THE TABLE

1. Read down from Player for the player's hand and down from Dealer for dealer's up card.
2. The case is given in plus or minus tens.
3. The Action column gives the reverse of the straight percentage chart. As long as the case is equal to the case listed or greater, the straight percentage action will be reversed.

NOTE: The case represents the count when one-half of the deck has been cased.

Splitting

In the table for splitting, only the situations given are worth learning. Other situations are not affected enough by 10's and aces to warrant changing the action. Sevens are left out entirely since all of the actions on the straight percentages chart for splitting them are too strong to be changed by the number of 10's.

Aces have as much effect as 10's when the player is trying to decide whether to split 10's, 9's, or 8's. For 6's, 3's, and 2's, the aces have little effect.

SPLITTING TABLE (Player Cases 10's)							
Player	Dealer	Case	Action	Player	Dealer	Case	Action
ace, ace	ace	2—	Hit	6, 6	6	any	Split
	10	2—	Hit		5	any	Split
	9	3—	Hit		4	any	Split
	8	3—	Hit		3	any	Split
	7	3—	Hit		2	1—	Split
10, 10	6	2+	Split	4, 4	6	1+	Split
	5	2+	Split		5	1+	Split
	4	2+	Split		4	1+	Split
	3	3+	Split		3	3+	Split
	2	3+	Split		2	3+	Split
9, 9	9	any	Split	3, 3	8	1—	Split
	8	3—	Stand		7	1+	Hit
	7	2+	Split		6	3—	Hit
	6	3—	Stand		5	3—	Hit
	5	3—	Stand		4	3—	Hit
	4	2—	Stand		3	2—	Hit
	3	1—	Stand		2	2—	Hit
	2	1—	Stand				
8, 8	ace	1—	Hit	2, 2	7	1+	Hit
	10	2+	Stand		6	4—	Hit
	9	3+	Stand		5	4—	Hit
	8	any	Split		4	3—	Hit
					3	2—	Hit
					2	2—	Hit

DIRECTIONS FOR READING THE TABLE

1. Read down from Player for the player's hand and down from Dealer for the dealer's up card.
2. The case is given in plus or minus tens.
3. The Action column gives the reverse of the straight percentage chart. As long as the case is equal to the case listed or greater, the straight percentage action will be reversed.

NOTE: The case represents the count when one-half of the deck has been cased.

The check questions will again be the best means for learning the splitting table, which is read in the same way as the previous tables. For example, when the player has two 3's and the dealer has an 8 up card, the player should hit if the case is even or plus 10's and split if the case is minus 10's.

CHECK QUESTIONS

The following questions are designed to give the player practice in deciding the correct play. Solve them by thinking first of the straight percentage, then of the strength of the situation, then of whether a plus or a minus in 10's will affect the action.

Insurance

1. The dealer has an ace showing, and the count is one ace and one plus after four cards have been seen. Should you insure?

   Answer: When only one ace has been cased, the count must be two plus.

2. If the dealer has an ace showing, and the count is two aces and one plus, should the player insure?

   Answer: Yes.

3. The dealer has an ace showing. If the count is four and even with about half the cards having been cased, should you insure?

   Answer: Even though the count is even for 10's, with all of the aces out, the count for insurance could be considered an even bet.

Hitting on Stiffs

1. The dealer has a 3 showing and the player has 13. If the count is two and one plus, what action should be taken?
   Answer: Stand.

2. The dealer has a 9 showing and the player has 16. If the count is two aces and two plus, what is the action?
   Answer: Hit.

3. The dealer has a 6 showing and the player has 12. If the count is two aces and two minus, what is the action?
   Answer: Hit.

4. The dealer has a 10 showing and the player has 14. If the count is two aces and three plus, what action should be taken?
   Answer: Stand.

5. The dealer has a 5 showing and the player has 12. If the count is two and two minus, what action should be taken?
   Answer: Hit.

6. The dealer has a 9 showing and the player has 15. If the count is three and two plus with only six or seven cards left, what is the action?
   Answer: Stand. (The weight of the count makes the two plus equivalent to six to eight plus.)

7. The dealer has an ace showing and the player has a 16. If the count is two and two plus, what is the action?
   Answer: Hit.

8. The dealer has a 10 showing and the player has 15. If the count is two and one plus with nine cards having been cased, what is the action?
   Answer: Hit.

9. The dealer has a 2 showing and the player has 15. If the count is two and two minus with about twelve cards left uncased, what is the action?
   Answer: Hit.

10. The dealer has an 8 showing and the player has 16. If the count is two aces and one plus, what is the action?
    Answer: Hit.

11. The dealer has a 4 showing and the player has 13. If the count is two and two minus, what is the action?
    Answer: Hit.

12. The dealer has a 7 showing and the player has 14. If the count is two aces and four plus, what is the action?
    Answer: Hit on all stiffs against dealer's 7 or 8.

13. The dealer has 3 showing and the player has 14. If the count is three aces and one minus with half the cards having been cased, what is the action?
    Answer: Stand.

14. The dealer has a 3 showing and the player has 16. If the count is two aces and one minus after two-thirds of the deck has been cased, what is the action?
Answer: Stand.

15. The dealer has an ace showing and the player has 13. If the count is two aces and three plus with half the cards having been cased, what is the action?
Answer: Hit.

16. The dealer has a 6 showing and the player has 16. If the count is one ace and four minus with twelve cards having been cased, what is the action?
Answer: Stand.

17. The dealer has a 4 showing and the player has 15. If the count is three aces and two minus with three-fourths of the deck having been cased, what is the action?
Answer: Hit. (The weight of the case makes the count equal to minus four.)

18. The dealer has a 10 showing and the player has 12. If the count is two aces and three plus in 10's with half the deck having been cased, what is the action?
Answer: Hit.

19. The dealer has a 2 showing and the player has 12. If the count is four aces and one plus with approximately fifteen cards left uncased, what is the action?
Answer: Stand.

20. The dealer has a 5 showing and the player has 14. If the count is two aces and three minus in 10's, what is the action?
Answer: Hit.

Doubling

1. The dealer has a 10 showing and the player has 11. If the count is two and two minus, what action should be taken?
Answer: Hit.

2. The dealer has a 9 showing and the player has 10. If the count is two and two minus, what action should be taken?
Answer: Hit.

3. The dealer has a 6 showing and the player has 9. If the count is two and two minus, what action should be taken?
Answer Double.

4. The dealer has a 5 showing and the player has soft 19. If the count is two and two plus, what is the action?
Answer: Double.

5. The dealer has a 6 showing and the player has soft 15. If the count is two and two minus, what is the action?
Answer: Hit.

6. The dealer has a 6 showing and the player has 8. If the count is three and one plus with about half the cards cased, what is the action?
Answer: Hit. (The aces are equal to 10's. Since the three means the number of aces that are out, then the count would actually be less than one plus when considering doubling.)

7. The dealer has a 2 showing and the player has 11. If the count is minus two, with three-fourths of the deck having been cased, what is the action?
Answer: Hit.

8. The dealer has 5 and the player has soft 20. If the count is one and two plus, what is the action?
Answer: Double.

9. The dealer has a 4 showing and the player has 8. If the count is two aces and two plus, what is the action?
Answer: Double.

10. The dealer has a 2 showing and the player has soft 18. If the count is three aces and two plus with two-thirds of the deck having been cased, what is the action?
Answer: Double.

11. The dealer has a 2 showing and the player has soft 16. If the count is two aces and two plus, what is the action?
Answer: Hit.

12. The dealer has a 4 showing and the player has 11. If the count is one ace and minus three with half of the cards having been cased, what is the action?
Answer: Double.

13. The dealer has a 5 showing and the player has soft 17. If the count is four aces and one minus with two-thirds of the deck having been cased, what is the action?
Answer: Double.

14. The dealer has a 3 showing and the player has 9. If the count is two aces and one plus with twelve cards having been cased, what is the action?
Answer: Double. (Must be a minus count to hit.)

15. The dealer has a 3 showing and the player has soft 20. If the count is two aces and plus two with half the cards having been cased, what is the action?
Answer: Double.

16. The dealer has a 4 showing and the player has soft 18. If the count is three aces and one plus with half the cards having been cased, what is the action?
Answer: Double. (Must be minus two to stand.)

17. The dealer has a 2 showing and the player has 10. If the count is one ace and two minus with a third of the cards cased, what is the action?
Answer: Double.

18. The dealer has a 3 showing and the player has soft 17. If the count is three aces and one minus with three-fourths of the cards having been cased, what is the action?
Answer: Hit.

19. The dealer has a 4 showing and the player has soft 13. If the count is four aces and one plus with twelve cards left uncased, what is the action?
Answer: Double.

20. The dealer has a 3 showing and the player has soft 19. If the count is one and two plus with half the cards cased, what is the action?
Answer: Double.

21. The dealer has a 9 showing and the player has 9. If the count is two aces and three plus with two-thirds of the deck having been cased, what is the action?
Answer: Hit.

22. The dealer has an 8 showing and the player has 11. If the count is two aces and two minus with half of the deck having been cased, what is the action?
    Answer: Hit.

Splitting

1. The dealer has a 9 showing and the player has two 9's. If the count is two and two minus, what is the action?
   Answer: Split.

2. The dealer has a 9 showing and the player has two 8's. If the count is three and three plus with about half the deck cased, what is the action?
   Answer: Stand.

3. The dealer has a 2 showing and the player has two 3's. If the count is three and two minus with about ten cards left uncased, what action should be taken?
   Answer: Hit.

4. The dealer has a 7 showing and the player has two 9's. If the count is two and one plus, what is the action?
   Answer: Stand.

5. The dealer has a 3 showing and the player has two 6's. If the count is two and one plus, what is the action?
   Answer: Split.

6. The dealer has a 5 and the player has two 9's. If the count is three and minus one with about twelve cards uncased, what is the action?
   Answer: Split.

7. The dealer has a 2 and the player has two 6's. If the count is two and one minus, what is the action?
   Answer: Split.

8. The dealer has a 10 showing and the player has two aces. If the count is two aces and one minus with half of the deck cased, what is the action?
   Answer: Split.

9. The dealer has a 6 showing and the player has two 10's. If the count is three aces and one plus with half the deck cased, what is the action?
   Answer: Stand.

10. The dealer has an ace showing and the player has two 8's. If the count is three aces and two minus, what is the action?
Answer: Hit.

11. The dealer has a 7 showing and the player has two 3's. If the count is one ace and one minus with twelve cards having been cased, what is the action?
Answer: Split.

12. The dealer has a 4 showing and the player has two 2's. If the count is two aces and two minus with three-fourths of the deck having been cased, what is the action?
Answer: Hit.

13. The dealer has a 5 showing and the player has two 4's. If the count is two aces and two plus, what is the action?
Answer: Split.

14. The dealer has an 8 showing and the player has two 9's. If the count is three aces and two minus with half the deck having been cased, what is the action?
Answer: Split.

15. The dealer has a 3 showing and the player has two 10's. If the count is one ace and two plus with twelve cards left un-cased, what is the action?
Answer: Split. (The case has a weight of 4 plus).

16. The dealer has a 2 showing and the player has two 8's. If the count is one ace and three minus, what is the action?
Answer: Split.

17. The dealer has a 7 showing and the player has two aces. If the count is three and one minus, what is the action?
Answer: Split.

18. The dealer has a 2 showing and the player has two 4's. If the count is two aces and three plus with half the deck cased, what is the action?
Answer: Split.

19. The dealer has a 7 showing and the player has two 9's. If the count is two aces and one plus, what is the action if half the deck has been cased?
Answer: Stand.

20. The dealer has a 2 showing and the player has two 3's. If the count is two aces and one minus, what is the action?
   Answer: Split.

General Questions

1. The dealer has a 5 showing and the player has 16. If the count is two and two minus, what is the action?
   Answer: Stand.

2. The dealer has a 4 showing and the player has 10. If the count is two and one minus, what is the action?
   Answer: Double.

3. The dealer has an ace showing and the player has 13. If the count is two and two plus, what is the action?
   Answer: Insure; then if the dealer does not have a blackjack, hit.

4. The dealer has a 6 showing and the player has two 8's. If the count is two and two minus, what is the action?
   Answer: Split.

5. The dealer has a 4 showing and the player has 12. If the count is two and two minus, what is the action?
   Answer: Hit.

6. The dealer has a 3 and the player has a soft 18. If the count is two and two plus, what is the action?
   Answer: Double.

7. The dealer has a 3 and the player has a 9. If the count is zero and one minus with six cards having been cased, what is the action?
   Answer: Double. (Weight of the count reduces case.)

7.

ADVANCED CASING

INTERMEDIATE BLACKJACK covers the straight percentages, which is the basis of good play, and beginning variations of the straight percentages by means of keeping track of 10's and aces. In this advanced section, casing the deck will be expanded to cover the 10's and aces, plus the high and low cards.

Like intermediate casing, advanced casing will use the same basic method. One out of three cards should be a 10. Advanced casing goes further by noting that one out of three should be a small card (2, 3, 4, or 5), and one out of three should be a medium card (6, 7, 8, or 9). Whenever an ace is seen, it is counted separately. Actually, only the 10's and small cards need be cased since the medium cards can be easily determined. For example, if the count is two plus in 10's and even in small cards, it would have to be two minus in medium cards.

Practice the count below and then use a deck of cards.

Example 1

7, 5, A, 3, (1 ace, 1+, 1−)   J, 6, 4, (2+, even)
4, 5, 9, (2+, 2−)   8, 3, 5, (3+, 1−)
7, A, K, 2, (2 aces, 2+, 2−)   3, K, 6, (3+, 1−)
2, 9, 7, (3+, 2−)   10, Q, K, (1+, even)
8, 6, 9, (4+, 1−)   4, 7, 8, (2+, even)
8, 10, Q, (3+, even)   10, 4, 2,(2+, 1−)
3, 9, A, Q, (3 aces, 3+, even)   A, Q, 10, J, (4 aces, even, even)
J, J, 5, (2+, even)

Example 2

4, 3, J, (even, 1−)   K, Q, 7, (1+, 2+)
Q, 8, 9, (even, even)   2, 5, 2, (2+, even)
8, 8, K, (even, 1+)   9, 9, Q, (2+, 1+)
6, 2, 6, (1+, 1+)   10, J, 3, (1+, 1+)
5, ace, 6, 7, (one ace, 2+, 1+)   4, 4, 4, (2+, 1−)
7, 2, ace, K, (2 aces, 2+, 1+)   Q, 10, ace, 10, (3 aces, even, even)
7, 5, K, (2+, 1+)   6, ace, J, 5, (4 aces, even, even)
8, 3, 10, (2+, 1+)   9, 3, J, (even, even)

Example 3

4, K, 4, (even, 1−)   10, 5, Q
5, 2, 10   2, 7, Q
8, 10, K   3, J, 2
6, Q, 9   ace, 7, 4, 9
3, 8, 5, (even, 1−)   K, 2, ace, 9
ace, 10, 6, J   7, 6, 6
J, 4, 3   8, 8, K
5, 3, 9   Q, ace, J, 7, (4 aces, even, even)

Note that in practicing with a full deck the ending will always be even and even after all cards have been dealt. This
method of casing the deck should be practiced with a deck,
turning up three cards at a time. When you get proficient enough
to go through the deck at a rapid pace and regularly end up
with the even and even count, you should practice the method
as if you were playing.

There is an alternate method for starting the count after the
dealer reshuffles. This is used when the dealer runs out of cards
after having dealt each player at least two cards. Instead of
starting over and recasing all exposed cards, as in intermediate blackjack, the count is reversed and all cards that have been
dealt to other players but not exposed will then have been already cased.

For example, if five people are playing and all have been dealt
two cards before the dealer runs out of cards, then the count is
reversed and all cards already dealt have now been cased. If the
count is three aces, two plus in 10's, and two minus in small
cards, then when the dealer runs out of cards the count is one
ace, two minus in 10's and two plus in small cards. The un-
exposed cards are already cased since the count, having been,
reversed, has taken them into consideration.

Whenever you are not certain that you have cased the cards accurately, use the method of recasing all exposed cards. The method of reversing the count was not used in intermediate blackjack because it is unlikely that a person just learning how to case cards will be accurate enough to make a running count for more than one deck. Even after you have become very accurate at casing, it would be wise not to go over two reshuffles without using the recasing method. Also, this new method can only be used when the dealer has dealt at least two cards to each player before reshuffling. If the dealer has dealt only one card to each player, it is impossible to determine which of the cards the reversal affected.

Do not reverse the count if your hand is pat, or if you can restart the case from the beginning after you have hit. If the count has been reversed and the dealer has collected cards from one or more players who broke on that hand, you should continue with the case as reversed, after taking his hit, unless the discards are recalled.

For practice, follow the new method of reversing the count and keeping track of the small cards. The aces are named first if an ace has just been exposed. Then the 10's, then the small cards.

K, 7, 4, (even, even)
8, 9, 3, (1+, even)
3, J, ace, 5, (1 ace, 1+, 1−)
8, K, ace, 7, (2 aces, 1+, even)
8, 2, 3, (2+, 1−)
5, Q, K, (1+, 1−)

10, 3, 7, (1+, 1−)
7, 4, 2, (2+, 2−)
5, Q, 9, (2+, 2−)
K, 10, 2, (1+, 2−)
2, Q, 8, (1+, 2−)
9, 5, 10, (1+, 2−)

Each player has been dealt two cards, and the dealer must now reshuffle. Therefore, the count should be reversed. Instead of (1+, 2-), it should be (1-, 2+), which means one minus in tens and two plus in small cards. Only two aces have been dealt; therefore it is still two aces. Had four aces turned up, the count would have been reversed to zero aces. As the dealer hits the player, these hit cards are cased. When the dealer turns the players' down cards over, you have the option of recasing from an even count or continuing with the reversed count, in which case the down cards have been cased by the reversing action. Try reversing the count in the following:

J, Q, 3   2, 10, Q
7, 2, 8   4, 4, 2
5, Q, 6   8, 10, 6
3, K, 9   4, 8, 3
ace, 6, ace, 9, J   3, K, 4
6, K, 2   (2 aces, 1+, 2−)

The players all have two cards and the first two players took a hit. If the dealer reshuffles, what is the new count? The answer is two aces, one minus, and two plus. You should start a new case when the hitting passes or if your hand is pat.

Remember that the reversing the count method can only be used in limited situations. These limits have been mentioned. They require two cards already dealt to each player before the dealer reshuffles, an accurately cased deck, and no more than two reshuffles before recasing. Although these limits restrict the use of this method, it can be a valuable tool because it gives the player a considerable advantage to know a sizeable portion of the deck on the first new hand after reshuffling.

Questions on Advanced Casing

1. In advanced casing, the medium cards are those from 4 through 7. True or False?

   Answer: False. Medium cards are 6, 7, 8, and 9. Small cards are 2, 3, 4, and 5.

2. If the count is two plus in 10's and one minus in small cards, then there are two extra 10's and one less small cards remaining. True or False?

   Answer: True.

3. The count for medium cards in Question 2 would be ——
   Answer: One minus in medium cards.

4. If the dealer deals every player a card before shuffling, the count that remains can be reversed when the dealer resumes dealing. True or False?

   Answer: False. The deal can only be reversed if each player has been dealt two cards or more.

5. The dealer deals each player two cards and the count is one ace, two minus in 10's, and one plus in small cards. If the dealer reshuffles, what is the count when play resumes?

   Answer: Three aces, two plus in 10's, and one minus in small cards. The down cards are not recased when the dealer exposes them unless the count is restarted.

6. Keep count: 8, 4, 7; 7, J, 9; 6, K, ace, 8; 9, 5, K; 4, 10, 7;
   Q, Q, 9; J, 5, 9; 8, ace, 2, 10; 2, 10, 2; ace, 7,
   Q, 6; J, 4, 10; K, 5, Q.
   The count is —aces, ——tens, ——small cards.
   Answer: Three minus aces, two minus tens, three plus
   small cards.

7. Keep count: 6, 7, 9; 4, 10, 5; J, 5, 7; ace, ace, Q, 10, 4;
   8, J, 8; 7, 2, 9; 2, 6, K; J, 8, ace, 3; Q, 10, K;
   3, 6, 3; 8, 3, 5; K, 6, 7; J, K, 9.
   The count is —aces, —tens, —small cards. The dealer
   shuffles; each of the four players has two cards; the dealer
   reshuffles and continues to hit the players: 9, 2, K. The
   count is —aces, —tens, —small cards.
   Answer: Three aces, even, two plus reversed to one ace,
   even, and two minus.

8. Should the case for Question 7 start back at zero aces, even
   and even if the player has a pat hand?
   Answer: Yes. (Recase all cards as they are turned up.)

9. Should the case for Question 7 start back at an even count
   if the player is able to recase all cards as they are seen after
   having reversed the count and taken a hit?
   Answer: Yes. (Start the case from the beginning when
   possible to insure accuracy.)

10. Practice with a deck of cards until counting becomes auto-
    matic.

Casino de Monte Carlo, the world's most famous gambling casino

8.

ADVANCED VARIATIONS

NOW THAT YOU have learned how to case the cards for advanced blackjack, you must make the casing work to your advantage. Although advanced casing is more difficult than beginning casing, the advanced variations are easier to learn than the beginning variations. This does not mean that beginning variations are not important. On the contrary, the doubling, splitting, and hitting on 14 is still dependent on the 10's count and beginning variations.

The importance of advanced casing and advanced variations can be seen by analyzing the stiff hands. The 12 and 13 stiffs are directly affected by the medium group (6, 7, 8, and 9), and the 15 and 16 stiffs are affected by the small group (2, 3, 4, and 5). The direct effect of the small and medium cards enables the player to play the stiffs more accurately than relying on the effort of the 10's count.

Advanced Blackjack Stiff Table

The advanced variations follow a logical pattern. When a situation comes up for the player either to hit or stand on a 12 or 13, the influence of the medium cards will determine the action to take. The player, by referring to the straight percentage table, will be able to determine what effect the medium cards will have on the action. The stiff table will show that one minus in medium cards will change the straight percentage action for the 12 against the dealer's 2 or 3 up card. If the count is one or more minus, the player should stand instead of taking a hit.

The 12 or 13 stiff when the dealer has a stiff up card makes a natural grouping to study. All that must be remembered is that half the situations need only one plus or one minus in medium cards to change the action, and that the other half needs 2 plus medium cards to change the action. The first half is for the 12 and 13 against the 2 or 3 up and the 12 against the 4 up. The second half is against the dealer's 6 or 5 up, and the 13 against the dealer's 4 up.

ADVANCED BLACKJACK STIFF TABLE (Player Cases 10's, Small Cards, and Medium Cards)							
Player	Dealer	Case	Action	Player	Dealer	Case	Action
12	2	1—M	Stand	12	7	any.	Hit
13	2	1+M	Hit	13	7	any	Hit
14	2	2—T	Hit	14	7	any	Hit
15	2	1+S	Hit	15	7	3—S	Stand
16	2	1+S	Hit	16	7	2—S	Stand
12	3	1—M	Stand	12	8	any	Hit
13	3	1+M	Hit	13	8	any	Hit
14	3	2—T	Hit	14	8	any	Hit
15	3	2+S	Hit	15	8	2—S	Stand
16	3	2+S	Hit	16	8	2—S	Stand
12	4	1+M	Hit	12	9	4—M	Stand
13	4	2+M	Hit	13	9	4—M	Stand
14	4	2—T	Hit	14	9	any	Hit
15	4	3+S	Hit	15	9	2—S	Stand
16	4	3+S	Hit	16	9	2—S	Stand
12	5	2+M	Hit	12	10	3—M	Stand
13	5	2+M	Hit	13	10	3—M	Stand
14	5	3—T	Hit	14	10	2+T	Stand
15	5	3+S	Hit	15	10	1—S	Stand
16	5	3+S	Hit	16	10	1+S	Hit
12	6	2+M	Hit	12	ace	4—M	Stand
13	6	2+M	Hit	13	ace	4—M	Stand
14	6	3—T	Hit	14	ace	any	Hit
15	6	3+S	Hit	15	ace	2—S	Stand
16	6	3+S	Hit	16	ace	2—S	Stand

DIRECTIONS FOR READING THE TABLE

1. Read down from Player for the player's hand and down from Dealer for dealer's up card.
2. The case is given in plus or minus tens (T), plus or minus small cards (S), or plus or minus medium cards (M). "Any" signifies that it would take too large of an overbalance to change the action.
3. The Action column gives the reverse of the straight percentage chart except when "any" is listed as the case. As long as the case is equal to the case listed or greater, the straight percentage action will be reversed.

NOTE: The case represents the count when one-half of the deck has been cased.

The 14 stiff will still depend on the 10 count, as in beginning variations. The player will hit against the dealer's 2, 3, or 4 with a two plus in 10's, and against a 5 or 6 up card with a three plus in tens.

The 15 and 16 stiff against the dealer's stiff up card is another natural grouping. Against a 2 up card it takes only a one plus in small cards to change the action to hit. Against a 4, 5, or 6 up card, a three plus in small cards is required to hit.

The 15 and 16 stiffs against the 7, 8, 9, 10, or ace is the grouping of most importance in the second part of the advanced stiff table. Against a 10 up card, the 15 stiff should be hit when the count for the small cards are even or plus. When the count is minus, the 15 should stand. The 16 stiff should be hit on a plus count for the small cards. The 15 and 16 stiffs, against the dealer's 8, 9, and ace up card, needs a two minus count for the small cards to stand.

The weight of the count for advanced blackjack is the same as for intermediate blackjack. The count is assumed to be taken when half the cards have been cased. The count is then multiplied by the weight as shown in the weight table.

WEIGHT TABLE

Number of Cased Cards (Less Aces)	Proportion of Deck Cased	Multiply Case by:
0	0	½
12	¼	⅔
24	½	1
32 (16 left)	—⅔	1½
36 (12 left)	—¾	2
46 (6 left)	—⅞	4

It should take only a short time for you to convert automatically the count to compensate for the weight. An approximation of the proportion of cards is all that is needed. For example, if you have only cased three or four sets of cards, you should think of the overbalance as being one half the strength of the actual case. A mathematical calculation is too difficult and of little or no value. If you are not certain as to the methods for finding the proportion of the deck cased, turn back to the last two pages of Chapter 5.

An example for using the weight table with advanced variations is as follows:

The player has 13 and the dealer has a 9 up card. If the count is two plus in 10's and one plus in small cards with about ten cards left uncased, then the count for the medium cards is three minus. With the two multiplier from the weight table, the count is worth six minus. The action would be to stand, since the table indicates to stand on four or more minus in medium cards.

Doubling

Most double down situations will depend on the 10's, just as in Intermediate Blackjack. The effect of small cards or medium cards will not be of sufficient importance to warrant a change in most doubling situations. For this reason, the doubling chart used for beginning variations in Chapter 6 will be similar to the doubling table used for advanced variations.

The 11, 10, 9, 8, soft 14, soft 18, soft 19, and soft 20 are not affected enough to alter the 10's count method by an over or under balance of small cards or medium cards.

A plus count in medium cards will improve your chances for doubling down on a soft 13 when the dealer has a 5 or 6 up card. The medium cards should be given equal weight as a 10 for these situations. For example, a one minus in 10's and a one minus in small cards would be equal to one plus in 10's when using the chart for soft 13. The medium count would be two plus, so added to the one minus in 10's leaves one plus.

The soft 15, soft 16, and soft 17 are affected by small cards, and the small cards count should be added to the 10's count against any stiff. For example, if you have a soft 16 (ace and a 5), you should double against a 2 up card if the count is one plus in 10's and two plus in small cards. The total, when using the double table in this situation, is three plus.

DOUBLING TABLE (Advanced Casing)							
Player	Dealer	Case	Action	Player	Dealer	Case	Action
11	ace	1−T	Hit	8	6	1+T	Double
	10	1−T	Hit		5	2+T	Double
	9	1−T	Hit		4	2+T	Double
	8	2−T	Hit		3	3+T	Double
	7	3−T	Hit		2	3+T	Double
	6	any	Double	Soft 13*	6	1−T	Hit
	5	any	Double	Soft 14	5	1−T	Hit
	4	any	Double	Soft 15	4	1+T	Double
	3	4−T	Hit	Soft 16	3	3+T	Double
	2	3−T	Hit		2	3+T	Double
10	ace	1+T	Double	Soft 17	6	3−T	Hit
	10	1−T	Hit		5	3−T	Hit
	9	1−T	Hit		4	2−T	Hit
	8	2−T	Hit		3	1−T	Hit
	7	3−T	Hit		2	1+T	Double
	6	any	Double	Soft 18	6	3−T	Stand
	5	any	Double		5	3−T	Stand
	4	any	Double		4	2−T	Stand
	3	4−T	Hit		3	2+T	Double
	2	3−T	Hit		2	2+T	Double
9	ace	any	Hit	Soft 19	6	3−T	Hit
	10	any	Hit		5	2+T	Double
	9	any	Hit		4	2+T	Double
	8	2+T	Double		3	2+T	Double
	7	1+T	Double		2	3+T	Double
	6	3−T	Hit	Soft 20	6	2+T	Double
	5	2−T	Hit		5	2+T	Double
	4	1−T	Hit		4	2+T	Double
	3	1−T	Hit		3	2+T	Double
	2	1−T	Hit		2	3+T	Double

DIRECTIONS FOR READING THE TABLE

1. Read down from Player for the player's hand and down from Dealer for dealer's up card.
2. The case is given in plus or minus tens.
3. The Action column gives the reverse of the straight percentage chart. As long as the case is equal to the case listed or greater, the straight percentage action will be reversed.

NOTE: The case represents the count when one-half of the deck has been cased.

* Count for medium cards can be added to tens' count against 5 or 6 when the player has soft 13.

Special emphasis should be spent on the study of the double down situations. These have double the importance of a single bet situation, since twice the amount of the original wager is involved. When the dealer has a stiff up card, and you pass up an opportunity to double, you are passing up the difference in percentage that is your advantage. If you have a 60 percent chance to win on a double situation, you are throwing away an extra $2 for each $10 wagered when you fail to double down.

Splitting

The splitting table for advanced variations will be similar to the one for beginning variations. There are only a few minor changes that need be noted. The changes are two 8's and two 6's.

(SPLITTING TABLE) (Advanced Casing)							
Player	Dealer	Case	Action	Player	Dealer	Case	Action
ace, ace	ace	2−T	Hit	6, 6	6	any	Split
	10	2−T	Hit		5	any	Split
	9	3−T	Hit		4	any	Split
	8	3−T	Hit		3	2+M	Hit
	7	3−T	Hit		2	1−M, T	Split
10, 10	6	2+T	Split	4, 4	6	1+T	Split
	5	2+T	Split		5	1+T	Split
	4	2+T	Split		4	1+T	Split
	3	3+T	Split		3	3+T	Split
	2	3+T	Split		2	3+T	Split
9, 9	9	any	Split	3, 3	8	1−T	Split
	8	3−T	Stand		7	1+T	Hit
	7	2+T	Split		6	3−T	Hit
	6	3−T	Stand		5	3−T	Hit
	5	3−T	Stand		4	3−T	Hit
	4	2−T	Stand		3	2−T	Hit
	3	1−T	Stand		2	2−T	Hit
	2	1−T	Stand				
8, 8	ace	1−T	Hit	2, 2	7	1+T	Hit
		1+S	Hit		6	4−T	Hit
	10	2+T	Stand		5	4−T	Hit
		2+S	Hit		4	3−T	Hit
	9	3+T	Stand		3	2−T	Hit
		3+S	Hit		2	2−T	Hit
	8	any	Split				

DIRECTIONS FOR READING THE TABLE

1. Read down from Player for the player's hand and down from Dealer for dealer's up card.

2. The case is given in plus or minus tens.
3. The Action column gives the reverse of the straight percentage chart. As long as the case is equal to the case listed or greater, the straight percentage action will be reversed.
4. "T" indicates tens, "M" indicates medium cards, "M,T" indicates total of medium and tens, "S" indicates small cards.

NOTE: The case represents the count when one-half of the deck has been cased.

The two 8's (16) should be hit when the dealer's up card is an ace and when the count is one minus in 10's or a one plus count in small cards. Reduction in 10's and additional small cards swing the percentages in favor of hitting rather than splitting. When the 10's and small cards are both plus or both minus, the 8's should be split, as the advantage for a plus in small cards is eliminated by a plus in 10's, and vice-versa.

You should hit two 8's against a 10 up card when the count for the small cards is two plus, and you should stand when the 10's count is two plus. When the dealer's up card is 9, you should hit the two 8's (16) when the count of the 10's is three plus or when that of the small cards is three plus.

Two 6's against a 3 up card should be hit when the medium count is two plus. Against a 2 up card, the 6's should be split with a minus count in medium cards or 10's.

Splitting, like doubling, must not be taken lightly. Failure to split when the odds are in your favor throws away your best single opportunity to gain an advantage over the dealer.

Insurance

The 10's count is the controlling factor for insurance just as it is in beginning blackjack. When the only ace that has been cased is the ace up card, a one plus count in 10's brings the odds even for insurance. When more than one ace has been cased, a one plus in 10's is a favorable advantage.

CHECK QUESTIONS

Advanced Variations

1. If the player has 15 or 16, what will affect the action—the tens, small cards, or medium cards?
   Answer: Small cards.

2. If the player has 14, what will affect the action?
   Answer: 10's.

3. If the player has 12 or 13, what will affect the action?

> *Answer*: Medium cards. The 10's and small cards must be added and the medium cards are the reverse. Example: Two plus in 10's and one minus in small cards will equal one minus in medium cards. Two plus in 10's and one plus in small cards will give three minus in medium cards. Two minus in 10's and one plus in small cards will give one plus in medium cards.

Hitting on Stiffs

1. Approximately half the deck has been cased and the count is two aces, one minus in 10's and 1 minus in small cards. If the player has 13 and the dealer has 4, what action should be taken?

> *Answer:* The reverse of the straight percentages. Hit instead of standing.

2. Approximately half the deck has been cased and the count is two aces, two minus in 10's, and three plus in small cards. If the player has 15 and the dealer has a 6 showing, what action should the player take?

> *Answer:* Hit instead of standing.

3. Approximately half the deck has been cased and the count is two aces, two plus in 10's and one plus in small cards. If the player has 13 and the dealer has 3, what action should be taken?

> *Answer*: Stand. The count indicates there are 3 minus in medium cards. Whenever the player has 12 or 13 and the dealer has a 2, 3, 4, 5, or 6, the medium cards must be plus in order to hit.

4. Approximately half the deck has been cased and the count is two aces, one minus in 10's and three plus in small cards. If the player has 16 and the dealer has a 6 showing, what action should be taken?

> *Answer*: Hit.

5. Approximately half the deck has been cased and the count is two aces, two plus in 10's, one minus in small cards. If the player has 15 and the dealer has 2, what action should the player take?

Answer: Stand. Always remember that, when the player has 15 or 16 and the dealer has a 2, 3, 4, 5, or 6, the small cards must be plus in order to hit.

6. Approximately half the deck has been cased and the count is two aces, one plus in 10's and two minus in small cards. If the player has 16 and the dealer has an 8, what action should be taken?
   Answer: Stand.

7. Approximately half the deck has been cased and the count is two aces, one plus in 10's and two plus in small cards. If the player has 12 and the dealer has 9, what action should be taken?
   Answer: Hit. Note that it takes a large over-balance in minus medium cards to reverse the hit situation for 12 or 13 to the dealer's 7, 8, 9, 10, or ace.

8. Two-thirds of the deck has been cased and the count is two minus in 10's and one plus in small cards. If the player has 14 and the dealer has a 3 up card, what action is required?
   Answer: Hit.

9. Half the deck has been cased and the count is one plus in 10's and even in small cards. If the player has 12 and the dealer has a 2 up, what action is required?
   Answer: Stand.

10. Approximately twelve cards are left uncased and the count is even in 10's and one plus in small cards. If the player has 16 and the dealer has a 3 up card, what action is required?
    Answer: Hit.

11. One-third of the cards have been cased and the count is one plus in tens and two minus in small cards. If the player has 15 and the dealer has 10, what action should be taken?
    Answer: Stand.

12. Half the deck has been cased, and the count is one plus in 10's and one minus in small cards. What action should be taken if the player has 15 and the dealer has 7?
    Answer: Hit.

13. Two-thirds of the deck has been cased, and the count is one minus in 10's and one minus in small cards. If the player has 13 and the dealer has a 5 up card, what action is required?
Answer: Hit.

14. Half the deck has been cased and the count is even in tens and one minus in small cards. If the player has 16 and the dealer has an ace, what is the action?
Answer: Hit.

15. Three-fourths of the deck has been cased and the count is one plus in 10's and two minus in small cards. If the player has a 12 and the dealer's up card is a 10, what action should be taken?
Answer: Hit. (The count must be 3 minus in medium cards to warrant a stand.)

16. Half the deck has been cased and the count is two plus in 10's and two minus in small cards. If the player has 14 and the dealer has an 8 up card, what action should be taken?
Answer: Hit. ("Any" means to hit on any count.)

17. Half the deck has been cased and the count is one plus in 10's and one minus in small cards. If the player has 15 and the dealer has a 9 up card, what action is required?
Answer: Hit.

18. When the player doubles on a soft 13 against a 5 or a 6 up card, the count for the medium cards should be added to the 10's count. True or False?
Answer: True.

19. Passing up a double down situation when the dealer has a stiff up card will cost the player twenty percent of the double wager in the long run if the player has a sixty percent advantage by doubling. True or False?
Answer: True.

20. If the count is two aces, one minus in 10's and two plus in small cards, what action is required if the player has two 8's and the dealer has a 10 up card?
Answer: Hit.

9.

DOUBLE DECK, THE SHOE, AND FINE POINTS OF PLAY

ADVANCED CASING is not the ultimate in playing blackjack. It is possible to case the deck more completely and make further adjustments to the advanced variation table. This chapter will describe the improvements that can be made, and miscellaneous items of importance.

Double Deck

Double deck blackjack is played with two decks of cards, with all cards dealt face up except the hole card. It is a much faster game than single deck blackjack. The players do not pick their cards up and the dealer does not have to wait as long for them to count the hand after a hit. Many of the large Nevada casinos play double deck blackjack because a greater number of games can be dealt without reshuffling.

The method for casing the deck, as presented in Chapter 5 and 7, can be used for double deck blackjack with greater accuracy than for regular blackjack. The fact that the cards are dealt face up makes the deck considerably easier to case. The player has more time to see the cards and does not have to case as fast as in regular blackjack. The grouping of cards in sets of three is also much easier.

DOUBLE DECK — WEIGHT TABLE

Number of Cased Cards, Less Aces	Proportion of Decks Cased	Multiply Count By
12	1/8	2/7
24	1/4	1/3
36	3/8	2/5
48 (48 left)	1/2	1/2
60 (36 left)	5/8	2/3
72 (24 left)	3/4	1
84 (12 left)	7/8	2
90 (6 left)	15/16	4

The weight table for double deck blackjack must be enlarged to include the extra deck of cards. The variation tables were calculated on the basis of twenty-four cards remaining. The regular weight table will not change when using the *quantity of cards remaining* as the basis for determining the multiplier.

As shown by the above weight table, the first part of the double deck will have a small multiplier. This indicates that the count must be high to be of value in using the variation table. With two decks of cards, the chances for a high over or under balance of cards are good.

The last part of the deal will give the player a decided advantage. With the higher counts possible and with standard multipliers, the count value will often have added importance.

Insurance for double deck blackjack should be taken when the count for 10's is more than one plus for every three aces left in the deck. The following table indicates the breakdown of aces to the count and the action to be played:

DOUBLE DECK INSURANCE TABLE

Number of Aces Remaining in Deck	Case (10's Count)	Action
7 aces	3 plus or more	Take Insurance
6 aces	3 plus or more	Take Insurance
	2 plus	Even Odds
4 or 5 aces	2 plus or more	Take Insurance
3 aces	2 plus or more	Take Insurance
	1 plus	Even Odds
1 or 2 aces	1 plus or more	Take Insurance
Zero aces	1 plus or more	Take Insurance
	Even	Even Odds

Players having trouble casing the deck for regular blackjack should try to find a double deck game. If the dealer doesn't reshuffle the cards before the end of the deck, the game will be much easier to case.

The Shoe

A shoe for dealing blackjack is used in many Las Vegas casinos. The shoe, a small black box with a slot in one end for releasing the cards, will generally hold four decks of cards.

The best way to play against a shoe is to place a minimum wager against the first two decks. The second two decks can be played at a higher wager, since the dealer will be unable to re-shuffle. The four decks of cards will have more lopsided counts than regular blackjack. If the player is placing higher wagers against the last two decks, he will have better overall odds. Casing the deck accurately from the start of play, and throughout all four decks, is the secret of success against the shoe. Insurance will be taken in the same manner as described for double deck blackjack.

Blackjack Machines

Early in 1965, a large number of automatic blackjack machines were sold throughout the state of Nevada. The machines have a minimum of twenty-five cents and a maximum of five silver dollars, five half dollars and five quarters.

The electronically operated machines have several disadvantages for the scientific blackjack player. The cards are re-shuffled after each hand, the player can't split pairs, doubling is limited to 10 or 11, and the machine is slow. The luxurious casinos which have installed the machines will probably take them out eventually.

Extension of Advanced Casing

The advanced casing method divides the deck into 10's, small cards and medium cards. If you are observant while playing, you can develop a knack for breaking the deck down further. The further breakdown need not be an accurate case, but merely an observation of the cards as they are played.

For example, if the count is two aces, one plus for 10's, and two minus for small cards, you might remember that none of the 9's has been exposed and most of the 7's and 6's have been played. The stiff table shows that you should hit a 14 when the up card is a 10, unless the count is two plus for 10's. By using blackjack logic, you should realize that the additional 9's and the few 7's and 6's remaining will hurt your chances for making a good hand and consequently you will not hit the 14. In a situation such as this, you should be able to gain an occasional extra advantage by noticing any unusual trends that might not show up in the regular casing.

The additional observation should not be attempted if it distracts from the regular casing. Obviously, you must be able to use blackjack logic, and you must know the variation tables thoroughly. The best cards to observe, in order to improve your chances, are the medium group of cards. It is more important to know the ratio of the 9's and 8's than the smaller cards.

The following examples demonstrate the applications of additional observation. They cannot, of course, cover every possible situation.

Example 1.

The count is one ace, even 10's, and one minus, small cards. You observe that most of the 5's and 6's have been played. If you have 15 and the dealer has a 9, you should stand. With additional 5's and 6's gone, you should realize that even though a small card count of two minus is needed for a stand situation, you have lost the primary small cards needed to beat a 19.

Example 2.

The count is two aces, even 10's, and even small cards. You observe that most of the medium cards have been 9's and 8's. If you have 11 and the dealer has a 9 up card, what action should you take? The doubling tables indicates to double down unless the count is one minus in 10's. In this situation the 9's and the 8's have nearly as much importance as a 10, so you should hit instead of doubling.

Example 3.

The count is one minus 10's and a one minus small cards. You observe that the 8's and 9's have appeared more than the 5's and 6's. If you have two 2's and the dealer has a 3 up card, should you split the 2's? Once again the tables say yes, but logic says no. The additional 5's and 6's will help the four count and the fewer 8's and 9's will hurt the splitting situation.

10.

TRAINING GAME

THE TRAINING GAME is a challenging contest between two or
more players or against par. It is designed to improve blackjack
playing ability and as a tuneup before playing in a casino.

Rules

One player acts as the dealer and deals two cards face down
to two, three, or four spaces. Two cards are turned face up, and
the dealer deals himself one card down and one card up.

The dealer hits the down hands with one or two cards each,
turned face up. There is no need to look at the hands to see if
they require a hit.

The hand that was turned face up is called the challenge
hand. The dealer has the option of selecting the hand as a challenge or to continue dealing until the appearance of a more
difficult situation. (See Chapter 17 for dealing sequence.)

When the dealer has designated the hand as a challenge, the
player must write on their sheet the case, the proportion of the
deck cased, and the action they would take for the challenge
hand. After all the players have written their answers, the
dealer makes an accurate case of all the exposed cards. The
method used for making the accurate case is explained below
under *Dealer's Case*.

The dealer's case is used for scoring. Three points are awarded if the player's case was correct. Two points are allowed if only the ace count was wrong. One point is allowed if either the 10's count or the small cards count was wrong·by one plus or one minus. No points are scored if the case was inaccurate by more than one plus or minus.

The exposed cards are counted for determining the proportion of the deck cased. If the player estimated the proportion within eight cards, one point is scored. A correct action earns three points.

After each challenge by the dealer, the cards are reshuffled, and the game is resumed. The first player to reach 100 points wins. If the game is played against players of uneven skill, or with only one player, then par can be used. Find par by adding up the total points possible and multiply by .90.

Sheet	1			SCORE SHEET					*Bill*	
No.	Player's Hand	Dealer's Up	Case	Pts	Weight	Pts	Actions	Pts	Total Points	Total Poss.
1.	14	3	3 1+/-	3	1/2	1	STAND	3	7	7
2.	10	8	2 1-0	2 2-0 /	1/4	1	Double	3	12	14
3.	9	10	3 1+/-	3	2/3	1	Hit	3	19	21
4.	15	10	1 2-0	3	3/4	1	Hit	3	26	28
5.	Soft 15	3	2 0 1+	2 1+/+ /	1/2	1	Double	0	28	35
6.	12	8	3 1+/1+	3	2/3	0	Hit	3	34	42
7.	3,3	5	1,3+,2-	3	1/4	1	SPLIT	3	41	49
8.	16	10	2,2+,1-	3	1/2	1	STAND	3	48	56
9.	10	10	2,1-2+	2 1-1/+ /	1/2	1	Hit	3	53	63
10.	12	2	0,0,2+	3	1/4	1	STAND	3	60	70
11.	9,9	7	1,1+1-	3	1/2	1	SPLIT	0	64	77
12.	15	9	4 2-0	3	7/8	1	Hit	3	71	84
13.	Soft 13	3	2 0 0	3	1/2	1	Hit	3	78	91
14.	16	10	3,2+2-	2 2+1- /	2/3	1	STAND	3	83	98
15.	12	3	1 3+0	3	1/4	1	STAND	3	90	105
16.	11	9	4 2-0	3	7/8	1	Hit	3	97	112
17.	16	7	2,2+1-	2,1-,1- /	1/2	0	Hit	3	101	119
18.										
19.										

Par — Total Poss. 119 x .9 — 107

Dealer's Case

An accurate case of the exposed cards can be made by separating them into groups of three. Each group should be arranged, when possible, with one 10, one medium card, and one small card. These even groups can be set aside and the remaining cards cased. The remaining cards should be grouped into threes at random. When one extra card is left at the end of the case, it should be considered as a plus.

For example, the last five cards, after the balanced groups are removed, are a 10 and four small cards. Grouping three small cards, the count is one plus 10's and two minus small cards. The remaining 10 and small card will increase the medium card total to two plus.

Examples

For Bill's first hand on score sheet Number 1, he had the correct count, so he received three points, plus one point for the right weight, and as his action was correct he scored another three points, for a total of seven points. On, the second hand, he had a count of two aces, one minus in 10's, and even in small cards. Upon casing the deck it was found to be 2, 2-, 0. He received only one point for casing since he was off by one minus. Had had been off by more than one minus, he would have received zero. His answers for the weight and the action were correct, giving him a total of five points for the hand.

In analyzing Bill's score, we find that he was six points short of beating par. His casing the deck was fair and should improve with practice. He missed two action plays that hurt him considerably since they were both double down situations.

The second example sheet shows that Bill improved his casing. He did not, however, improve on the double down situations. All things considered, Bill did an excellent job of casing and he played at better than even odds.

No.	Player's Hand	Dealer's Up	Case	Pts	Weight	Pts	Actions	Pts	Total Points	Total Poss.
1.	14	3	31°1-	3	1/2	1	STAND	3	7	7
2.	10	8	2,1-0 $^{2\ 2\text{-}0}_{1}$		1/4	1	Double	3	12	14
3.	9	10	31+1-	3	2/3	1	Hit	3	19	21
4.	15	10	12+0	3	3/4	1	Hit	3	26	28
5.	Soft 15	3	201+ $^{2\ 1+\ 1+}_{1}$		1/2	1	Double	0	28	35
6.	12	8	31+1+	3	2/3	0	Hit	3	34	42
7.	3,3	5	1,3+2-	3	1/4	1	Split	3	41	49
8.	16	10	2,2+1-	3	1/2	1	STAND	3	48	56
9.	10	10	2,1-2+ $^{2\ 1\text{-}1+}_{1}$		1/2	1	Hit	3	53	63
10.	12	2	0,0,2+	3	1/4	1	STAND	3	60	70
11.	9,9	7	1,1,+1-	3	1/2	1	Split	0	64	77
12.	15	9	4,2+0	3	7/8	1	Hit	3	71	84
13.	Soft 13	3	200	3	1/2	1	Hit	3	78	91
14.	16	10	3,2+2- $^{2\ 2+/\text{-}}$		2/3	1	STAND	3	83	98
15.	12	3	13+0	3	1/4	1	STAND	3	90	105
16.	11	9	42+0	3	7/8	1	Hit	3	97	112
17.	16	7	2,2+1- $^{2,1\text{-}1\text{-}}_{1}$		1/2	0	Hit	3	101	119
18.										
19.										

Sheet 2 — SCORE SHEET — Bill

Par — Total Poss. 112 x .9 — 100

Alternate Methods of Play

Double down and splitting can be worth six points if the players want to add importance to these situations. This will give the player added incentive to learn the all-important double down and splitting situations accurately.

If the training game is played using intermediate blackjack instead of advanced blackjack, the casing should be worth only one or two points.

11.

CALCULATIONS

THE CALCULATIONS in preparing the tables and graphs for this book were made without the aid of a computer or even an adding machine. I used a slide rule, logic, and hard work. Although I have had college math courses through differential and integral calculus only adding, dividing, and multiplying were needed.

My first step was to make up an estimated straight percentage table through logic. I was then faced with calculating the various situations to prove or disprove the estimates. It took me about eight hours to make my first calculation. After ten situations were calculated, the time was cut down to two to three hours each. As the calculations were made, I kept revising the table to correct mistakes in my initial estimates.

Once the straight percentage table was accurate, I put my calculations into graphs such as graph 1A and 1B in Chapter 6. By combining these graphs with logic, I then estimated the intermediate variations table. By following this table, I calculated each action, proving or disproving the actions. Since the graphs were a good guide for making the intermediate table, the table was remarkably accurate before calculations. This accuracy saved me many hours since it usually takes two calculations to prove each action. If many of the estimates had been off by more than one plus or minus, many more calculations would have been necessary.

As I now had many charts, graphs, and tables to follow, it was a reasonably quick procedure to make the preliminary variations table for advanced blackjack. More work of the same kind produced the advanced table.

Each situation for the advanced variations could be almost infinitely calculated to take into account the exact number of cards seen, the exact case, the effect of the entire case, etc. But this, I felt, would be much too bulky to be of a practical use. Instead, I chose to list only the portion of the case that had the greatest effect on the *action*. Even though some accuracy is lost by simplifying the advanced table to such an extent, the loss is insignificant.

Procedure Used For Calculations

There are three major steps which I used to calculate each action. The first step was to calculate the dealer's percentage for a 21, 20, 19, 18, 17 or to break. The second step was to calculate the player's percentages for various actions that could be taken. The third step was to integrate the player's percentages with the dealer's in such a way as to show the percentage that the dealer will win, the percentage of push, and the percentage the player will win.

For the remainder of this chapter, I will use an example of one calculation that was made for determining an action for the advanced variations table. For this particular situation, the player will have a 16 and the dealer will have a 4 up card. Through the use of the straight percentage table, we know that the player should stand on the 16. The intermediate variations table shows that he should hit the 16 if the count is 4 minus in 10's. The four minus in 10's indicates that there are two plus in small cards and two plus in medium cards. The two plus in small cards is the logical factor that will determine if the player should hit. For this reason, I had a (2+S) for the case needed to change the straight percentage from stand to hit. To prove this action I made the calculations for standing and hitting.

Dealer's Percentages

For all calculations, I used a situation in which half the deck was cased—that is, twenty-six cards. Two of the remaining cards are aces.

Dealer Has A 4 Up Card

Case = 2+S (7 Tens, 7 Medium, 10 Small Cards) (7 Tens, 1.75 each Medium Card, 2.5 Each Small Card)								
Multi-plier	Hole Card	2 Cards	21	20	19	18	17	Break
2	ace	5	3.5	3.5	3.5	3.5	—	—
2.5	2	6	—	—	—	—	—	—
2.5	3	7	—	—	—	3.5	17.5	—
2.5	4	8	—	—	3.5	17.5	3.06	—
2.5	5	9	—	3.5	17.5	3.06	3.06	—
1.75	6	10	3.5	17.5	3.06	3.06	3.06	—
1.75	7	11	17.5	3.06	3.06	3.06	3.06	—
1.75	8	12	3.06	3.06	3.06	3.06	4.38	12.25
1.75	9	13	3.06	3.06	3.06	4.38	4.38	15.32
7	10	14	12.25	12.25	17.5	17.5	17.5	73.50
26.0			42.87	45.93	54.24	58.61	55.99	101
Chances out of 26			1.65	1.77	2.09	2.25	2.16	3.89

The multiplier for the above calculations indicates the chances out of twenty-six cards for the dealer to have the corresponding hole card. The multiplier is multiplied by the chance of hitting a corresponding card to make 21, 20, 19, 18, 17, or break. The chances to hit a 21, 20, etc., are then added and divided by twenty-six. This gives the average chance of hitting the 21, 20, 19, 18, 17, or break.

Multiplier	3 Cards	2nd Hit					
		21	20	19	18	17	Break
2	6	5	5	5	5	—	—
10	7	5	5	5	5	70	—
16.2	8	5	5	32.4	113	28.3	—
22.5	9	5	45	158	39.4	39.4	—
28.7	10	57.4	201	50.2	50.2	50.2	—
32	11	224	56	56	56	56	—
34.5	12	60.3	60.3	60.3	60.3	86.2	242
37	13	64.7	64.7	64.7	92.5	92.5	324
39.5	14	69	69	98.7	98.7	98.7	415
63	15	110	157.5	157.5	157.5	157.5	772
63.8	16	159.5	159.5	159.5	159.5	127.6	893
349.2		764.7	828	847.3	873.8	806.4	2646
Chances out of 26		2.19	2.37	2.43	2.50	2.31	7.37

Multiplier	4 Cards	3rd Hit					
		21	20	19	18	17	Break
—	7	—	—	—	—	—	—
2.2	8	5	5	—	15	4	—
6.2	9	16	6	44	11	11	—
11.5	10	12	80	20	20	20	—
18.3	11	128	32	32	32	32	—
26.2	12	49	49	49	49	49	183
34.0	13	59	59	59	85	85	297
41.8	14	73	73	104	104	104	439
49.8	15	87	125	125	125	125	611
73.2	16	183	183	183	183	140	1025
263.2		612	612	616	624	587	2555
Chances out of 26		2.33	2.33	2.34	2.37	2.23	9.69

Dealer's Accumulated Percentage

1ST HIT

$1.65/26 - 21 = .0636$
$1.765/26 - 20 = .0680$
$2.09/26 - 19 = .0805$
$2.25/26 - 18 = .0867$
$2.155/26 - 17 = .0830$ .... .3818
$3.89/26 - Break = .1495$ .... .1495

2ND HIT

$12.2/26 \times 2.19/26 - 21 = .0395$
$.469 \times 2.37/26 - 20 = .0428$
$.469 \times 2.43/26 - 19 = .0439$
$.469 \times 2.50/26 - 18 = .0451$
$.469 \times 2.31/26 - 17 = .0417$ .... .2130
$.469 \times 7.57/26 - Break = .1365$ .... .1365

3RD HIT

$.469 \times 6.63/26 \times 2.33/26 - 21 = .0107$
$.1192 \times 2.33/26 - 20 = .0107$
$.1192 \times 2.34/26 - 19 = .0107$
$.1192 \times 2.37/26 - 18 = .0109$
$.1192 \times 2.23/26 - 17 = .0102$ .... .0532
$.1192 \times 9.69/26 - Break = .0444$ .... .0444

Sub Total .... .9784
21, 20, 19, 18, 17 = .0024 .... .0120
Break = .0096 .... .0096
Total 1.0000

TOTALS
21 = .1162
20 = .1239
19 = .1375
18 = .1451
17 = .1373
Break = .3400

Total = 1.0000

From here on the calculations are simpler. The player's percentages are not nearly as difficult since there is only one hit necessary. The player's percentages for hitting are as follows:

$$
\begin{aligned}
21, 20, 19, 18 &= .0962 \text{ each} = 9.62\% \text{ each} \\
17 &= .0769 = 7.69\% \\
\text{Break} &= .5383 = 53.83\%
\end{aligned}
$$

Here is an integration of the dealer's percentages and the player's percentages:

Dealer Wins (%)		Push (%)		Player Wins (%)	
Players	**Dealers**	**Players**	**Dealers**	**Players**	**Dealers**
.3655 × .1162		.0962 × .1162		.0962 × .5438	
.2693 × .1239		.0962 × .1239		.0962 × .4199	
.1731 × .1375		.0962 × .1375		.0962 × .2824	
.0769 × .1451		.0769 × .1373		.0962 × .1373	
.0425				.0523	
.0333		.0112		.0404	
.0238		.0119		.0272	
.0112		.0132		.0132	
.1108		.0140		.1331	
.5383		.0106		.1569	
.6491		.0609		.2900	

The bottom numbers in the above chart show the final percentages for the hit situation. The dealer will win 64.9 percent of the time and the player will win 29 percent of the time. They will push 6.1 percent of the time.

The percentages when the player stands are 34 percent in favor of the player and 66 percent in favor of the dealer. The player will lose a difference of 32 percent to the dealer if he stands. If he hits he will lose 64.9 percent, less 29 percent, or 35.9 percent. The player should stand since he will lose a lower overall percentage.

The calculation proves that the two plus for small cards was not enough overbalance to change the action from standing to hitting. Therefore, it was necessary to make another calculation that showed that a three plus for small cards was needed to change the action.

GLOSSARY OF BLACKJACK TERMS

Broke or Bust. Having a total count of 22 or more.

Burned Card. The first card following the shuffle and cut is usually turned face up under the last card. A card that was turned up by mistake may also be burned by placing it on the bottom of the deck.

Double Deck Blackjack. Blackjack played with two decks and dealt face up.

Double Down. Doubling the wager after receiving cards, but before receiving another hit card. The player turns his cards face up and receives one hit card face down.

Hard Hand. Any hand that does not have an ace counted as 11.

Hit. Asking for another card.

Insurance. Betting that the dealer has a blackjack when he has an ace up card. The player is allowed to place a wager equal to or less than half the original wager. Insurance plays two to one.

Peeking. The dealer looks at the top card in the deck. Peeking is used by crooked dealers in conjunction with dealing seconds.

Pit. The areas of a casino where the dealers and the bosses (called pit bosses) stand.

Push. Tie between player and dealer. The player neither wins nor looses.

Scratching. Asking for a hit by scratching the table with the cards.

Seconds. Dealing the second card from the top instead of the first card. To cheat in this manner requires the dealer to peek at the top card.

Shoe. A container holding several decks of cards from which the dealer slips out one card at a time.

Soft Hand. A hand that includes an ace, which can be counted as either one or 11 without going over 21.

Splitting. When a player has two cards of the same count, he may separate them and double his wager. If aces are split, he receives only one card face down on each. Any other split pair may be hit as many times as desired.

Stiff. Any hand that totals 12, 13, 14, 15, or 16.

Third Baseman. The player on the lefthand side of the table. He is the last player to be able to ask for a hit.

Up Card. The dealer's card that is dealt face up.

PART TWO
COMPLETE CASINO GUIDE

12.

CRAPS

THIS CHAPTER on craps and the succeeding chapters on other casino games are presented to show the rules of the games and the percentages favoring the house. Unlike blackjack, craps and most other casino games do not require skill, but the player should at least learn the correct way to play in order to reduce the odds against him.

Craps is played with two dice and on a crap table, as shown in the illustration. There are usually three dealers and one or two box men. It is the dealer's job to take the bets and make payoffs to winners, and the box men back up the dealers by helping on payoffs, changing bills into chips, and overseeing the game in general.

Object

The crap layout shows many types of wagers that can be made. The most popular is *on the line*. The player bets that the shooter will roll a 7 or an 11 on the first throw of the dice. If 7 or 11 turns up, the dealer pays the line bets one for one, but·if a 2, 3, or 12 is thrown, the wager is lost. All other numbers becomes the shooter's point, and the dice are thrown until either the point or a 7 appears.

If the point is thrown before the 7, the line bets are paid one for one, but if the 7 is thrown first, then the line bets are lost. Losing by throwing a 2, 3, or 12 on the first roll of the dice, or

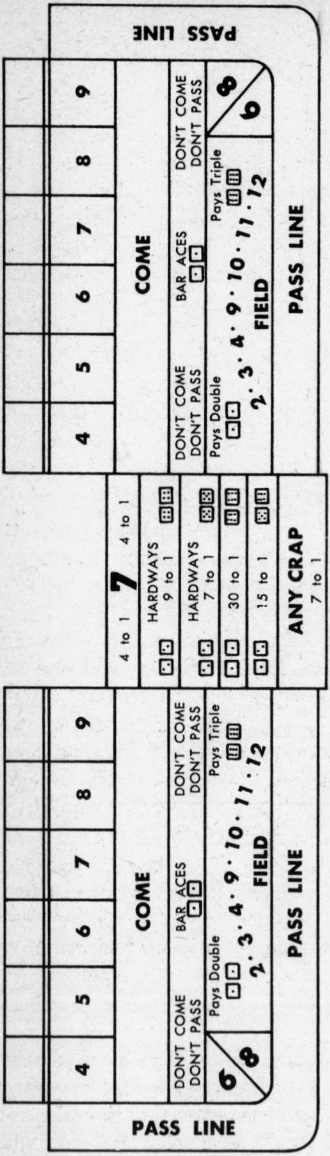

PASS LINE

4	5	6	7	8	9

COME

DON'T COME / DON'T PASS

BAR ACES

DON'T COME / DON'T PASS

Pays Triple

FIELD

2 · 3 · 4 · 9 · 10 · 11 · 12

Pays Double

PASS LINE

6 8

HARDWAYS

4 to 1   7   4 to 1

HARDWAYS   9 to 1

HARDWAYS   7 to 1

30 to 1

15 to 1

ANY CRAP

7 to 1

PASS LINE

4	5	6	7	8	9

COME

DON'T COME / DON'T PASS

BAR ACES

DON'T COME / DON'T PASS

Pays Triple

FIELD

2 · 3 · 4 · 9 · 10 · 11 · 12

Pays Double

PASS LINE

6 8

PASS LINE

CRAP LAYOUT

losing by throwing a 7 when trying for a point, is called *crapping out*. A *pass* is the term for making the point.

Line (1.4141 percent house advantage)

The *line*, as described in the preceding paragraph, is the first section on all crap layouts. The only time you should place a wager on the line is when the shooter is coming out with a new point. Occasionally a player will place a wager on the line while the shooter is trying for a point. This is a mistake since the player is losing the opening chance to win with a 7 or 11.

Normally the dealers and box men will advise the player that he is making an error. When a player does not know if the shooter is coming out with a new point, he should check the marker in front of the dealer. If the shooter is coming out, the marker will be off the layout and will have "off" written on the top of it. When the shooter is trying for a point, the marker is on the number with the "on" end showing.

Come (1.4141 percent house advantage)

The *come* section on the layout is exactly the same as the line, except that you are coming out with a new point before the shooter has completed his pass.

For example, if the shooter has thrown a 9 on his first throw, his point will be 9. After this first roll, you can place a new wager on the come line. If 7 or 11 is rolled, the come bet wins, and if a crap is rolled, the come loses. If a 4, 5, 6, 8, 9, or 10 is rolled, the number becomes the point for the come bet, and the dealer places the wager on the appropriate numbered box. When the come bet is won, it is returned to the come line and is paid off.

You should be alert to remove any portion of your wager and winnings as desired. The point for each come bet is separate from the line bet and is not affected by the line bet in any way. As in the line bet, the come point is lost when a 7 is rolled.

Don't Pass — Don't Come (1.4026 percent house advantage)

The *don't pass* and the *don't come* are nearly the reverse of the *line* or *come*. You take the side of the house against the line bet with the exception that you have either the 2 or the 12 barred from you on the first roll. If the 12 is barred, then you will neither win or lose if that number is rolled on the first throw.

When a wager is placed on *don't pass* or the *don't come*, you win on a roll of 2 or 3 on the first roll and will lose on a 7 or 11 (barring the 12). Once a point is rolled, you are betting with the house that the shooter throws a 7 before his point.

Crap game in progress

Place Bets (1.5151 to 6.6667 percent house advantage)

Place bets on 4, 5, 6, 8, 9, or 10 may be made at any time. The odds against these numbers vary, and the payoffs vary.

If you place a wager on 4, 5, 9, or 10, you should wager in increments of five; if you bet on a 6 or 8 place, you should wager in increments of six. You win a place bet any time the number placed comes up before a 7 is thrown. The 4 or 10 place pays nine for each five wagered; the 5 and 9 place pays seven for each five wagered; the 6 and 8 place pays seven for each six wagered.

The way to make a place bet is to give the dealer the wager and tell him the number to be placed.

Taking The Odds (zero house percentage)

Taking the odds is the best bet in craps, since the house does not have an advantage.

To take the odds you must first make a front line wager (come or pass) or a back line wager (don't come or don't pass). You can then place a wager on the point rolled at the exact odds.

Like the place bet, the wager should be in the correct increments to simplify the payoffs. For the front line odds, the 4 and 10 may be wagered in increments of one and the house pays two for one. The 5 and 9 should be in increments of two so that the wager can be paid three for two. The 6 and 8 should be in increments of five, so that the wager can be paid six for five. For the back line odds the wager should be in increments of two for the 4 and 10 to pay one for two. For the 5 and 9, the wager should be in increments of three to pay two for three. For the 6 and 8, the wager should be in increments of six to be paid five for six.

CALCULATIONS FOR DON'T PASS, TAKING DOUBLE ODDS
$1 IS WAGERED FOR 36 COME OUT ROLLS.

The "2" Is Barred For Don't Pass

Shooter's Point	Times Rolled	Odds to Win	Odds to Lose	$ Win	$ Lost
2	1	Barred	Barred	Barred	Barred
3	2	All	None	2.00	
7	6	None	All		6.00
11	2	None	All		2.00
12	1	All	None	1.00	
4	3	6/9	3/9	2.00	1.00
5	4	6/10	3/10	2.40	1.60
6	5	6/11	3/11	2.73	2.27
8	5	6/11	3/11	2.73	2.27
9	4	6/10	3/10	2.40	1.60
10	3	6/9	3/9	2.00	1.00
24 Chances For Double Odds,				24.00	24.00
TOTAL				$41.26	$41.74

(If carried to 6 decimal places, the amount won would be 41.254544 and the amount lost would be 41.745454.)

X = Casino's Edge

$$X = .005915 = \underline{\underline{0.5915\%}}$$

The limit for taking the odds will depend upon your front line or back line bet, the casino maximum limit, and the casino rules. Nearly all casinos will allow players to take single odds, which is the amount equal to twice the back line wager for 4 and 10. One and a half times his back line for 5 and 9 and one and one-fifth times the back line for 6 and 8. Many of the Lake Tahoe casinos, Reno casinos, and Sparks casinos will allow double odds. Double odds are twice the single odds shown above.

To illustrate a wager when taking the odds, let us suppose a shooter has made the point 5 on his opening throw. If you have made a wager of $6.00 on the pass line, you may take the odds with $2.00, $4.00 or $6.00 for single odds, or if double odds are allowed, any wager up to $12.00 may be placed. The procedure is to set the *odds* wager in back of the pass line wager and call out to the dealer that it is an odds wager. If the shooter makes the point, then you receive even money for the line wager and one and one-half times the *odds* wager.

The house percentage for a *don't pass* wager and *full double odds* is the best overall odds a player can find in craps. The house advantage is only .5915 percent. The calculation for the house percentage for the *don't pass, taking double odds,* is shown above.

Field (2.5641 percent house advantage)

A wager on the field is either won or lost on each throw of the dice. If the dice come up 3, 4, 9, 10, and 11, the player is paid one for one. If a 2 is rolled, he is paid two for one, and if a 12 is thrown he is paid three for one, or 2 to 1 depending on the casino. The wager is lost if the dice come up 5, 6, 7, or 8. If the field pays only two for one on both the 2 and the 12, the house percentage is more than doubled.

Big 6 or Big 8 (9.0909 percent house advantage)

The wager is exactly like a place bet except that the player does not benefit from the odds. The bet pays only one for one on the Big 6 or Big 8, whereas a place bet on the same number is paid seven for six.

Any Crap (11.1111 percent house advantage)

The player is betting that a 2, 3, or 12 will be thrown on one roll of the dice. The payoff is seven for one although the odds are nine to one.

Hardways (9.09 to 11.11 percent house advantage)

There are four hardway numbers, 4 (two 2's), 10 (two 5's), 6 (two 3's), and 8 (two 4's). The hardway number must come up in these pairs before any other combination of that number is rolled, or before a 7 is rolled.

Proposition Bets (11.11 to 13.89 percent house advantage)

Proposition bets are *one roll* longshot wagers on the 2, 12, 11, or 3. Perhaps the most popular use of these numbers is when *toking* (tipping) the dealer. Instead of giving a dealer a single tip, many players will play it for the dealer on one of these proposition numbers. Thus if the number is rolled, the dealer makes a substantial tip.

Wager	Odds	Casino Pays	Casino's Percentage
Pass or Come	18.255 to 17.745	1 to 1	1.4141
Don't Pass or Don't Come	17.745 to 17.255	1 to 1	1.4026
4 or 10 Place	2 to 1	9 to 5	6.6667
5 or 9 Place	3 to 2	7 to 5	4.0000
6 or 8 Place	6 to 5	7 to 6	1.5151
Pass Line Plus Single Odds	30.255 to 29.745	1 to 1 + Odds	.8485
Pass Line Plus Double Odds	42.255 to 41.745	1 to 1 + Odds	.6060
Don't Pass Plus Single Odds	29.745 to 29.255	1 to 1 + Odds	.8320
Don't Pass Plus Double Odds	41.745 to 41.255	1 to 1 + Odds	.5915
Field*	20 to 19	1 to 1	2.5641
Big 6 or Big 8	6 to 5	1 to 1	9.0909
Any Crap	8 to 1	7 to 1	11.1111
Hardway 4 or 10	8 to 1	7 to 1	11.1111
Hardway 6 or 8	10 to 1	9 to 1	9.0909
11 or 3 Proposition	17 to 1	15 to 1	11.1111
2 or 12 Proposition	35 to 1	30 to 1	13.8889
Any 7	5 to 1	4 to 1	16.6667

* The Field is calculated for the most popular layout where 2 pays double, 12 pays triple and the 3, 4, 9, 10, and 11 pays 1 to 1.

13.

ROULETTE

ROULETTE is the most popular casino game in Europe and one of the least popular games in the United States.

The reason for the difference in popularity is due to the difference in the layouts. The American layout has thirty-six numbers and two zeros whereas the European layout has thirty-six numbers with one zero or none at all. Even though Roulette offers the player relatively poor odds in the United States, the game is still played in most Nevada casinos. Women are the most frequent players in this country because roulette is a slow game and easy to understand.

The roulette layout as shown in the illustration is a typical American layout. The house advantage for this table is 5.263 percent. In Monte Carlo and most European casinos, where the layout has only one zero, the player loses only 1.351 percent to the house. The single zero and the *prison rule* accounts for the lower percentage.

Wagers placed on any section paying one to one can be placed in *prison* when the ball lands on zero, or the player can withdraw half the wager and lose the other half. The *prison* alternate means the wager is carried over to the next turn, and if the player wins he can withdraw the entire wager.

The markers on the layout show that a bet may be placed by covering any combination of numbers. It is common for players to purchase stacks of checks (chips) which can be wagered anywhere on the board. Each location has a minimum and a maximum wager. Most Nevada casinos allow the player to buy a stack of checks worth a minimum of ten cents per check. The player must generally place at least fifty cents on the layout for each turn. The most common maximums for any payout is five hundred dollars. European casinos often have a maximum payout of two thousand dollars or the equivalent.

Monte Carlo's roulette table in one of the salons privés (private rooms) where many of the world's millionaires have played.

In addition to designated areas to place wagers, the player may place checks on the lines between numbers, on corners, etc. The illustrated layout shows the payoffs. When a wager is placed on an outside line, the wager is covering numbers the entire width of the layout. When placed on inside lines, the wager is covering only the numbers touched. For the most part, the layout is self-explanatory.

The house percentage for roulette is the same for all wagers, except when placing the five-way bet on the zero, double zero, 1, 2, and 3. This bet can only be made on the American layout, since in Europe only one zero or no zeros are used. A five-bet cannot be payed at the same odds as all other wagers, because five will not divide into thirty-six evenly like all other wagers. Consequently the house will take the advantage.

American version of roulette

American Name	French Name	Payoff	American Odds	One Zero European Odds	No Zero Belgium Odds
Red & Black High or Low Odd or Even	Rouge-Noir Passe-Manque Impair-Pair	1 to 1	5.263	2.703 or (1.351 Prison Rule)	2.5
Dozens Or Column	Douzaine Or Colonne	2 to 1	5.263	2.703	2.5
6 Numbers	Sixain	5 to 1	5.263	2.703	2.5
5 Numbers	None	6 to 1	7.895	None	None
4 Numbers	Carre	8 to 1	5.263	2.703	2.5
3 Numbers	Transversale	11 to 1	5.263	2.703	2.5
2 Numbers	Cheval	17 to 1	5.263	2.703	2.5
1 Number	Enpleine	35 to 1	5.263	2.703	2.5

Systems

Roulette seems to attract the system player more than any other game. Most system players like the large variety of wagers possible, and by using the checks, they can spread the checks over as many numbers as they desire. This allows the player to increase his wagers at a more gradual rate than on other types of games. The progressive system then can be used with as slow a progression as the player might like. For a systems player with a small bank roll, the slow system on the slow game of roulette is appealing.

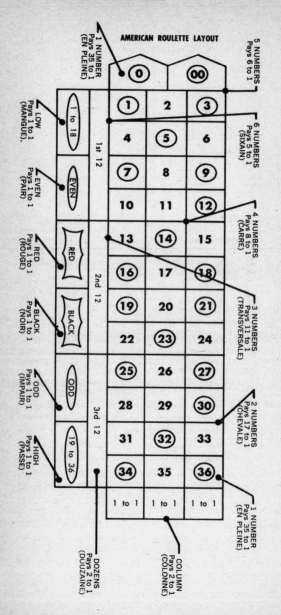

AMERICAN ROULETTE LAYOUT

14.

KENO

KENO IS ONE of the most popular games in Nevada gambling —this in spite of percentages which highly favor the house.

The cost of playing Keno can be relatively low at the same time as it offers the possibility of a large payoff. Keno winners are less apt to spend their winnings on gambling. Consequently, there are occasional big winners who bring the winnings home. This is always good advertisement and helps explain its popularity.

The game is played with a cage or hopper containing eighty numbered table tennis balls. A Keno dealer draws twenty of the balls, one at a time, and calls out each number as it is drawn and lights it up on a Keno board.

Before the game is played, the players mark the numbers they select to play on a Keno ticket that has the Keno layout printed on it. The most common number of selections are the 8 spot, the 8 spot special, and the 9 spot ticket—although the player can mark from 1 to 15 numbers. *Spot* is the terminology for marking a number. After a player has marked a ticket, he gives it to a Keno dealer who rewrites it. The dealer then stamps both tickets and keeps the player's original and gives the player the duplicate.

After the game has been played, the player checks the numbers marked on his ticket with the numbers on the Keno board. The payoff is made according to a schedule that is nearly the same in each casino. The following is an example of a typical payoff schedule:

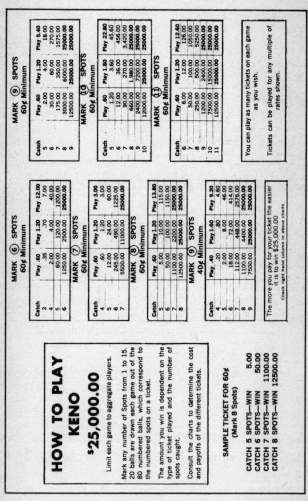

HOW TO PLAY KENO
$25,000.00

Limit each game to aggregate players.

Mark any number of Spots from 1 to 15. 20 balls are drawn each game out of the 80 numbered balls, which correspond to the numbered spots on a ticket.

The amount you win is dependent on the type of ticket played and the number of spots caught.

Consult the charts to determine the cost and payoffs of the different tickets.

SAMPLE TICKET FOR 60¢
(Mark 8 Spots)

CATCH 5 SPOTS—WIN   5.00
CATCH 6 SPOTS—WIN   50.00
CATCH 7 SPOTS—WIN   1100.00
CATCH 8 SPOTS—WIN 12500.00

MARK (6) SPOTS
60¢ Minimum

Catch	Play .60	Play 1.20	Play 12.00
3	.35	.70	7.00
4	2.00	4.00	40.00
5	60.00	120.00	1200.00
6	1250.00	2500.00	25000.00

MARK (7) SPOTS
60¢ Minimum

Catch	Play .60	Play 1.20	Play 3.00
4	.60	1.20	3.00
5	12.00	24.00	60.00
6	245.00	490.00	1225.00
7	5500.00	11000.00	25000.00

MARK (8) SPOTS
60¢ Minimum

Catch	Play .60	Play 1.20	Play 13.80
5	5.00	10.00	115.00
6	50.00	100.00	1150.00
7	1100.00	2200.00	25000.00
8	12500.00	25000.00	25000.00

MARK (9) SPOTS
40¢ Minimum

Catch	Play .40	Play 1.60	Play 9.20
4	.20	.80	4.60
5	2.00	8.00	46.00
6	18.00	72.00	414.00
7	112.00	448.00	2576.00
8	1100.00	4400.00	25000.00
9	7500.00	25000.00	25000.00

The more you pay for your ticket the easier it is to win $25,000.00
Check right hand column in above charts

MARK (9) SPOTS
60¢ Minimum

Catch	Play .60	Play 1.20	Play 5.40
5	30.00	60.00	270.00
6	30.00	60.00	270.00
7	175.00	350.00	1575.00
8	3000.00	6000.00	25000.00
9	12500.00	25000.00	25000.00

MARK (10) SPOTS
60¢ Minimum

Catch	Play .60	Play 1.80	Play 22.80
5	1.20	3.60	45.60
6	12.00	36.00	456.00
7	90.00	270.00	3,420.00
8	660.00	1,980.00	25000.00
9	2400.00	7200.00	25000.00
10	12000.00	25000.00	25000.00

MARK (11) SPOTS
60¢ Minimum

Catch	Play .60	Play 1.20	Play 12.60
6	6.00	12.00	126.00
7	50.00	100.00	1050.00
8	250.00	500.00	5250.00
9	1200.00	2400.00	25000.00
10	7500.00	15000.00	25000.00
11	12500.00	25000.00	25000.00

You can play as many tickets on each game as you wish.

Tickets can be played for any multiple of rates shown.

Typical Keno schedule

Keno stories are probably more often repeated than any other kind in gambling. A $25,000 win is remembered and publicized for years, and even the smaller amounts are generally good for much publicity. The best known of all winnings came from a $25,000 ticket written in a downtown Las Vegas casino. The casino safeguards against cheating were poor, and the winning ticket was supposedly a forgery. After a long legal battle, the casino did not have to pay, but the Keno game was closed by the gaming board for poor payoff policy.

Cheating by the casino is rare in Keno, although possible. When a wire cage is used, the Keno dealer can manipulate the balls as they are selected by announcing the wrong ball or by mechanically passing a ball up. Even some of the air-operated rabbit-ear types can be manipulated by flipping a ball out as it starts to enter the ears.

The most fool-proof hopper of all is the rabbit-ear type developed by Lyles Luke, at the Stardust Hotel in Las Vegas. This hopper has a positive slide arrangement that prevents the dealer from tampering with the selection. The advantage to the casino of tampering is rather slight since the dealer would have to remember specific tickets being played or else try to distribute the numbers evenly over the layout to cut down on the group type winnings. The 20 percent and plus casino edge makes this an unlikely game to be rigged.

15.

SLOT MACHINES

THE KING of low-cost gambling is the slot machine. For as little as a nickel, the player can pull a lever and watch the wheels spin. When the wheels stop on a jackpot payoff, a bell might ring, a light glows, and the player often yells "Jackpot!" or "Yippy!" at the top of his lungs. All this might seem a bit childish to sophisticated gamblers, but to thousands of players it is the most enjoyable game in the casino.

Reno and downtown Las Vegas for years have been the largest slot machine centers in the world, but the south shore of Lake Tahoe is fast becoming the big glamor spot for the slot player. With casinos like Harrahs Club, Harvey's Wagon Wheel Hotel, and the fabulous Sahara Tahoe Hotel furnishing the slot players with approximately 1,000 slot machines each, the machine has taken on a new importance in gambling. With the fierce competition between casinos for the slot machine business, the house advantage against the player is often small, and this is contributing to the increase in business.

Slot Machine Operation

Most slot machines have three reels, and each reel has twenty symbols. The machine payout, or house advantage, depends on the payoff quantity, the number of types of symbols, and the combination of symbols on each reel. There are thousands of combinations of symbols that can be placed on the reels, and by varying the payoff amount for each type of symbol an infinite number of ways can be made to vary the house advantage. When the payout is high, the machines are described as loose, and when the payout is low, the machines are described as tight.

Slot machines with their insides exposed

Two types of slot machines

The most common types of symbols used on slot machines, and their payout in coins, is shown by the following chart:

Symbol	1st Only	1st & 2nd	1st, 2nd & Bar	All Three—5¢ Slot	
Cherry	2	5	5	10	$ .50
Orange	0	0	10	10	.50
Plum	0	0	14	14	.70
Bell	0	0	18	18	.90
Bar*	0	0	—	150 or 100	7.50 or 5.00
7**	0	0	0	300 or 200	15.00 or 10.00
Lemon	0	0	0	0	0
Melon	0	0	150 or 100	150 or 100	7.50 or 10.00

* or the name of casino
** or the casino emblem

The Palace King slot machine shown in the photo has no lemons and has only six types of symbols. The pay-back to the customer for this Palace Club machine is 94 percent. This should give a clue as to what to look for when selecting a machine. With only six types of symbols, no lemons, and the full payoffs, the chances are good that the machine will pay back a high rate of return. On a slot machine such as this, the windows are large and the player can see a good part of the reel. The player, after a few coins, should be able to see the approximate number of jackpot symbols.

The machine shown in the top photo are the latest in automatic slot machines. They will take up to 1,000 coins at one time. This eliminates the need to feed in one coin at a time after each pull of the handle. The jackpot is paid off automatically in 25 seconds, thus eliminating a longer delay while waiting for a pay-off. Safety devices prevent the player from making an error by pulling off a jackpot before it is fully paid.

Payout Percentages

The payout percentages for slot machines vary from a high of 94 or 95 percent to under 50 percent.

The low payout machines are generally found in Nevada drug stores, grocery stores, and casinos that do not depend on the slot machine business. A casino paying back an average of 92 percent for slots is generally considered a competitive casino.

16.

MISCELLANEOUS CASINO GAMES

Baccarat-Chemin de fer

BACCARA AND CHEMEN DE FER are slightly different games in Europe, but in Las Vegas they are combined and known as Baccarat-Chemin de fer.

Las Vegas has only six Baccarat-Chemin de fer tables as of this writing. In Europe Baccara is second to roulette in popularity. European Baccarat is known as Baccara or Baccara a' Deux Tableux. The limits are generally higher for these games than for others. The Las Vegas limit is usually two thousand dollars and European limits are the approximate equivalent, although no limit games are common.

Baccara, as played in Europe, has a fixed bank. The bank is either the casino or the highest bidder. The game is played with six decks of cards and dealt from a shoe. The banker deals one hand to his left, one to his right, and one to himself.

Chemin de fer differs from Baccara in that the bank travels to the right each time the banker loses. The banker deals only one hand to the player with the highest wager and one hand to himself. The amount of the bank depends on the amount the banker puts before him. If one of the players calls "banco," he is betting against the entire bank, and the remaining players are merely bystanders.

Baccara tables at the Kursaal d'Ostende, Europe's largest casino

The Las Vegas Baccarat-Chemin de fer game uses eight decks of cards, and the shoe moves to the right from player to player, as in Chemin de fer. The game is dealt with only one hand to the player and one hand to the bank. The players have the option of betting with the bank or with the player, much the same as the *pass* line and *don't pass* line in craps. The house collects all losing wagers and pays the winning wagers. The house deducts 5 percent of the winnings on wagers for the bank to win.

The object of the game is to come closest to the number 9. The ace counts one, the deuce counts two and so on. The 10 and all face cards count zero. Two cards are dealt from the shoe to the player with the largest wager, and two cards to the person acting as banker. The shoe moves to the player on the right each time the acting banker loses. The player has the option of passing the shoe.

The game is played strictly according to the rules card. Both the player and the banker must play their cards exactly as shown on the rules card with no alternatives. If the player has an 8 or a 9, he turns the cards over. The player wins if the banker does not tie or beat the player's 8 or 9. If the banker has an 8 or a 9 and the player does not, the player loses without being able to draw. The player is always first to act. If the rule calls for a draw (third card), the player or banker must take their third card. A tie hand is the same as a *push* in blackjack, and is played over.

BACCARAT — CHEMIN DE FER
RULES

Player

Having	Action
1-2-3-4-5-10	Draws A Card
6-7	Stands
8-9	Natural (Banker cannot draw)

Banker

Having	Draws When Giving	Does Not Draw When Giving
3	1-2-3-4-5-6-7-9-10	8
4	2-3-4-5-6-7	1-8-9-10
5	4-5-6-7	1-2-3-8-9-10
6	6-7	1-2-3-4-5-8-9-10
7	Stands	
8-9	Natural (Player Cannot Draw)	

Pictures and 10's count zero.

If the player does not take a card, the banker stands on 6.

The Big Six

Many casinos in Nevada have one or more Big Six wheels. This game is easier to play than roulette, and although it has high house percentages, it can be quite fascinating. The large wheel turning slowly around has a magnetic effect on most players.

The Wheel of Fortune is one of the most common names given to a large vertical wheel. The proper names for the wheels in Nevada are either the Money Wheel or the Big Six. Although there is a difference between these two wheels, most casinos call either of the wheels a Big Six. The wheel showing dollar bills from one to twenty denominations, a card bearing a flag or the casino's name, and the joker is the most exciting.

Layout

A typical Big Six (money wheel type) shows on the wheel twenty-four $1 bills, fifteen $2 bills, seven $5 bills, four $10 bills, two $20 bills, one flag or casino name, and a joker. The layout has one each of these items encased in glass.

Payoff

The player places a minimum wager of 25 cents on any of the bills or cards. The $1 bill has a one to one payoff, the $2 bill a two to one payoff, and so forth. The joker and the other insignia pay forty to one, but the wager must be on the winning insignia to be paid.

Insignia Or Bill	Mathematical Odds	Casino Pays	Casino's Advantage
$1 Bill	53 to 24	1 to 1	11.1%
$2 Bill	53 to 15	2 to 1	16.7%
$5 Bill	53 to 7	5 to 1	25.9%
$10 Bill	53 to 4	10 to 1	18.5%
$20 Bill	53 to 2	20 to 1	22.3%
$ Joker	53 to 1	40 to 1	24.1%
$ Flag	53 to 1	40 to 1	24.1%

This layout is only one of many different layouts found in Nevada. When the wheel has fifty divisions instead of fifty-four, the odds change considerably, but the $1 bill remains the best bet. The $10 bill is the worst wager on the smaller wheels where there are only three $10 bills shown.

Winners Despite the Odds

Even though the casino advantage is high, there have been a few cases where players have legally eliminated the casino advantage and turned the advantage in their favor. The biggest winners of this type in my experience were a drummer and a bass player who were appearing in the lounge at the Dunes Hotel.

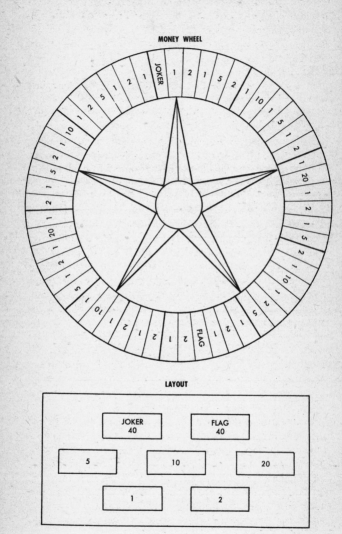

MONEY WHEEL

LAYOUT

These two musicians could time every wheel in Las Vegas to within eight divisions. This meant that they could wait for a turn to come near the joker, the flag, or the $20 bill and play for the high payoffs at odds of approximately seven to one. At the time they were playing, most Big Six dealers allowed the players to bet after the spin. The dealers turned the wheel only two or three spins, so it was hardly noticeable that the two musicians were timing the wheel.

They not only could judge the wheel accurately, but they worked as partners to distract the dealers and pit bosses. One would stand near the flag and the other near the joker. When they knew the wheel was going to stop in the area of the joker, the player standing near the flag would cause a distraction. The player near the joker would slide one or two $5 chips on the joker. If the wheel stopped on the joker, they won the forty to one payoff for approximately seven to one playing odds. After their first two weeks of play, Las Vegas Big Six dealers were no longer allowing bets after the spin of the wheel, but the two musicians were still able to get late bets down on occasions. The drummer was probably the biggest winner in Big Six history.

Like the players who timed the wheel, it is even easier for the dealer to turn the wheel so that it stops in a specific section. Although most casino managers give instructions to spin the wheel several times, the wheel can be spun so as to land in any half or any quarter of the area. This is an additional advantage for the casino if the dealer is keeping the forty to one payoffs away from the players. Fortunately, most Big Six dealers spin without looking at the wheel or timing its action.

Chuck-A-Luck

Chuck-a-luck is still played in two of the Nevada casinos and in the future it may appear in additional casinos. The game is of minor importance because it is seldom played for high stakes.

Chuck-a-luck is played with three dice which are turned in a bird cage having a central pivoting point. The dealer turns the bird cage over and the dice fall to the bottom. The players place wagers on a layout similar to the illustrated design.

Although there are a limitless number of designs possible, the one shown here is typical. Four different types of bets can be placed. The single number wagers pay one to one if one of the dice comes up with the number wagered, two to one if two dice come up with the correct number, and three to one if all three come up with the number.

CHUCK-A-LUCK

1	2	3	4	5	6
6	5	4	3	2	1

3 4 5 6 7 13 14 15 16 17 FIELD pays 1 to 1		
HIGH (above 10)	JACKPOT any 3 of a kind pays 30 to 1	HIGH (above 10)
LOW (below 11)		LOW (below 11)

high-low lose on 3 of a kind

The house advantage for the individual number wagers are 7.87 percent, for the field it is 15.7 percent, for the jackpot wager it is 13.89 percent, and for a high or low wager it is 2.78 percent. Although the high and low bets are best, the other types receive as much play. Most players are not aware of the percentages and they are more liable to play at the poor odds because there are three types of high house percentage bets and only one, the high-low bet, is at a low house advantage.

Faro

Faro is famous because it was once a favorite gambling game in the days of the wild west. Western movies and novels have helped to glorify Faro. Today the game is of minor importance to the gambling industry aad to the vast majority of players.

The lack of popularity of Faro is not due to the casino advantage. On the contary, a patient player can play Faro at low house odds. The lack of popularity of Faro compared to blackjack, craps and roulette are matters of enjoyment, economics, and difficulty. The complexity of Faro requires that a person spend considerable time in learning the method for wagering. Economically, Faro is an expensive game for a casino to operate, because it requires three persons to run the game and only a few players can play with any degree of comfort. Since most players play at low house advantage, the minimum wager is usually high with encouragement to purchase a stack of chips for $25 or more to enter the game.

Equipment

The Faro layout includes thirteen large cards representing the ace, 2, 3, 4, 5, 5, 7, 8, 9, 10, jack, queen, and king of spades. A high card area is printed on the layout. A standard playing deck of cards is dealt from a dealing box. A rack with markers representing the cards in the deck is used to case the cards as they are played.

Fundamentals of Play

The dealer shuffles the deck of cards and has a player cut the deck. It is then placed up in the dealing box. The dealer removes the top card, called the soda, and places it two spaces from the box. This card is similar to burning the top card in blackjack. The card now exposed in the dealing box is a winning number and this card is placed on top of the soda. The next card shown is the losing number. These two cards complete the first of twenty-five turns. The dealer casing the cards will move the markers in the rack to represent the winning and losing cards, as well as the soda. When the bets are payed, collected, or replaced, the dealer removes the losing card and places it next to the winning stack. The winning card for the second turn is now placed on the winning stack leaving the losing card in the dealing box. The game continues in this manner, until the twenty-five turns are played.

The betting on the Faro layout is tricky because the placement of the chips on the number indicates the type of wager being made. Placing chips on the center of a card indicates a bet for the number to win. Placing a marker on top of the wager is a bet for the number to lose. A split is defined as a number that comes up on both the win card and the lose card. The house collects half of each wager on that number. Combination bets on more than one number can be made by placing chips on various locations of the layout. This method of wagering logically should only be made on denominations that have the same case count. The only advantage of a combination bet is to enable the player to cover more numbers with a single wager and so speed up play.

Importance of the Case

Since each card is cased as it is exposed, the players know the number of cards remaining for each denomination. The house advantage comes from collecting one half of the wager on splits. This makes the house advantage zero when there is only one card of a denomination.

It is customary for the players to place a wager before any of the denominations are down to only one card. The best odds for each turn will be on the denominations that have the most cards removed from play.

Last Three Cards

The last three cards in Faro can be played in several ways. A number can be bet to win or lose, high or low, or on the order for the cards to appear, which is known as calling the turn. Calling the turn pays four to one, for five to one odds (a poor wager).

If two of the last three cards are a pair, it is known as a cat-hop, and the player can wager on the position of the odd card at two to one odds and no house advantage.

Odds for Faro

On the first wager after the cards have been shuffled, if the player bets on the same denomination as the soda, the house advantage is only 0.79 percent. If he bets on a denomination other than the soda, the odds are 1.57 percent in favor of the house. The house percentage will change for each denomination after each turn.

As previously mentioned, as long as the player places a wager on the denomination that has the most cards removed from play, he will be playing at the lowest possible odds. These odds should seldom be higher than 1 percent and most of the time the player will have even odds. If the player places a single bet when the best denomination has two cards remaining and combination bets when there is only card remaining, then he will have approximately five win or lose plays out of the twenty-five turns.

Only one of these plays will be at a house advantage. The overall house advantage will average about a quarter of 1 percent when played in this manner.

Boule

Boule or La Boule is played in most French and Swiss casinos. The game is similar to roulette except there are only nine numbers on the wheel. The dealer spins the ball around the wheel until it drops into a numbered slot.

The players can bet on individual numbers or on odd (red) or even (black). The house advantage for the odd and even wager is 11.1 percent. When the casino pays the individual numbers at seven to one, the house advantage remains the same, but when the payoff is six to one (as in Switzerland) the house advantage is 22.2 percent. Despite these heavy odds, Boule is popular due to the low minimum wager.

BOULE LAYOUT

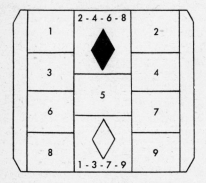

Trente et Quarante (30 to 40)

Trente Et Quarante is played at Monte Carlo, at the Casino Municipale in San Remo, Italy, and in a few other European casinos. The game has a very slim house advantage which is probably the reason it is not played in many casinos.

The game is played with six decks of cards shuffled together and placed in a shoe. The dealer places the cards in two rows, the upper row being known as *noire* (black) and the lower row being known as *rouge* (red). Each row must show a point count of 31 to 40, the ace counting one point, the picture cards ten points, and the remainder their numerical value. The winning row is the one that totals 31 or nearest to 31. When both rows total 31, it is called refait and the house collects half of all wagers.

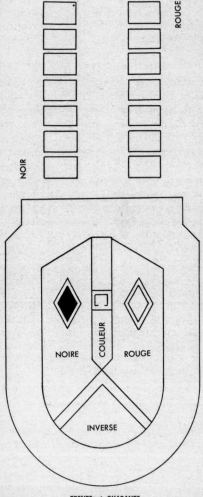

TRENTE et QUARANTE

Bets can either be placed on *noire* or *rouge,* or they can be placed on *couleur* or *inverse*. *Couleur* and *inverse* is determined by the first card of the *noire* row. If this card is red, the *couleur* wins if the *rouge* row wins. If the card is black, then the *couleur* wins if the *noire* row wins. Inverse wagers win when the color of the card is opposite to the color of the winning row. The player can insure against a refait by paying a premium of one percent. The minimum and maximum wagers are approximately $3 to $1,500 at San Remo, and $1 to $2,000 at Monte Carlo.

Other Casino Games:

Bingo, poker, and Pan are played in some casinos, but they hold a minor role in the casino picture. These games are usually played in a separate room or area, away from the other casino games. Poker and Pan do not need much introduction since the rules and the house take are much the same in casinos as they are in card rooms. The bingo games are played in the same way as regular bingo games, except that play is usually much faster.

The much publicized bingo games at Harrah's clubs in Reno and Lake Tahoe are perhaps the fastest of all bingo games. Harrah's Club in Reno has bingo going almost continuously at such a fast pace that the players hardly have enough time to dump the markers before the next game is started. Games are played for a $12 pot, and fifteen free games, with every fifth game being played for $15.

The house advantage varies with each game, since the number of players might vary from a small number of players to as high as 140 players. At 30 cents a game, the house advantage is a very high 200 percent or more when all the seats are filled. When only half the seats are filled, the odds are still worse than the regular casino games.

17.

HOW TO SHUFFLE AND DEAL

THERE ARE almost as many people interested in learning the mechanics of dealing as there are in learning the fundamentals of good playing. The style of shuffling and dealing presented in this chapter is the standard method used by professional black-jack dealers. It is not only faster and looks smoother than ama-teur methods, but it also does a better job of mixing the cards without exposing them.

The Shuffle

A fast shuffle takes a professional dealer about one and a half seconds. It takes seven seconds to complete two shuffles, four cuts, and another shuffle. Most amateur-type shuffles require twice the time, do not mix the cards as well, and often expose cards.

To learn the fundamentals of shuffling, practice on a well-padded, felt table. Dining room table pads are perfect; the pad allows the fingers tips to pick up bottom cards cleanly. A hard surface tends to increase fumbling. A new deck is undesirable, since the cards slip around.

The shuffle will be illustrated in seven steps. These steps are performed slightly differently by various dealers, but all are es-sential.

The first step in dealing is to divide the deck into two parts. As shown in Figure 1, the deck is set flat on the table. The bot-tom half of the deck is firmly gripped by the second and third finger on one side and by the thumb on the other side. The other hand grips the top half in the same way. The deck is then pulled apart in two halves. The index fingers are used to steady the top card for each half. This is especially important when the cards are slick. The little fingers are used at the ends of the deck to keep it square.

When the deck has been pulled apart, the ends should be butted together, keeping the deck square at all times with the little fingers doing all the butting. As shown in Figure 2, the index fingers are firmly keeping the top card from sliding. This is the second step.

The deck is momentarily set flat on the table in two halves as the hands shift into the third step. As shown in Figure 3, the middle joints of the small fingers are set on the outside corners of the deck.

Fig. 1. Shuffle *All photographs of card dealing sequence by Roland Pleterski*

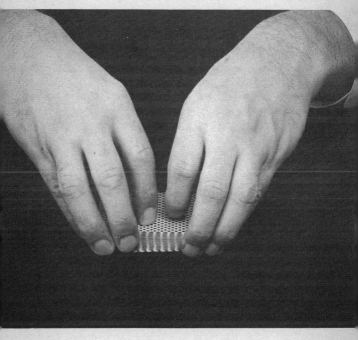

Fig. 2. Shuffle

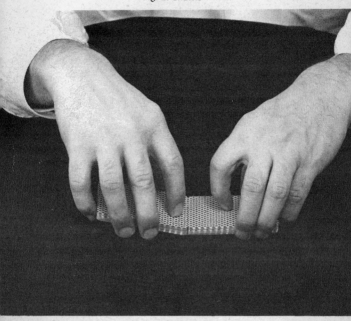

Fig. 3A. Shuffle

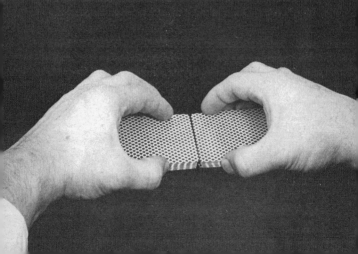

Fig. 3B. Shuffle

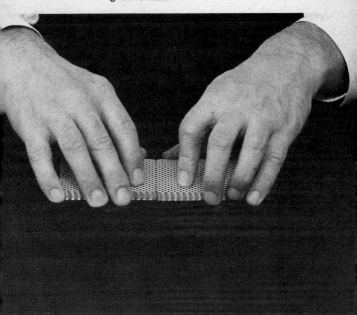

Fig. 4. Shuffle

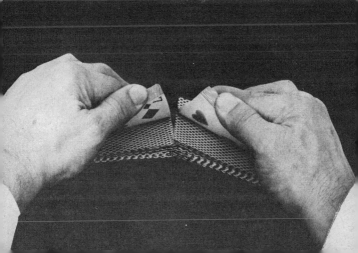

The outside corners are the pivot points for the fourth step. The thumb tips are positioned on the bottom of the deck, approximately half an inch in from the butting ends of the deck. This step number 4 is the most critical part of the shuffle because the cards won't mate if the two halves of the deck are not pivoted and fanned properly. Figure 4 shows the thumbs doing the lifting and releasing of cards. It also shows the two halves of the deck at an angle to each other. This angle was made by pivoting the cards toward the center as the cards are lifted. The sides of the little fingers keep pressure on the far outside corners so that the deck will not slip from the pivot point. The second and third fingers help the thumbs fan the cards. *Fanning* means to spread the cards so that the thumbs will have a wide area for releasing the cards evenly. The cards are released by lifting the thumbs. If properly fanned, the cards will fall smoothly from both parts of the deck.

Figure 5A shows the position of the fingers for the push together in the fifth step. This is accomplished by placing the little fingers behind each end of the deck, the second and third fingers on the front side, as close to the end as possible, and the thumbs on the back side. The little fingers do most of the pushing since they have all the leverage and can keep the cards even. The index fingers keep the top cards from sliding. The cards are pushed together as far as possible (Figure 5B) with one push. This straightens the deck back into alignment.

The last part of the push, the sixth step, is accomplished as shown in Figure 6A. The middle fingers are used to push and square the ends, and the thumbs keep the deck steady. The middle fingers move in a petting motion from outside in. Figure 6B shows an alternate method to square the deck. The right hand does the work and the left hand holds the deck stationary. This offers the advantage of better deck control.

Fig. 5A. Shuffle

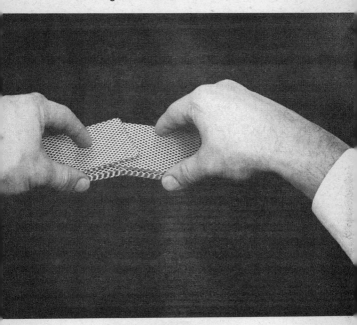

Fig. 5B. Shuffle

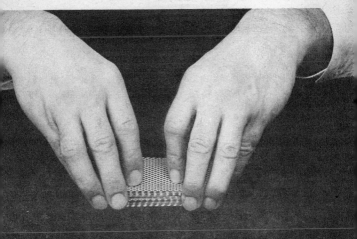

Fig. 6A. Shuffle

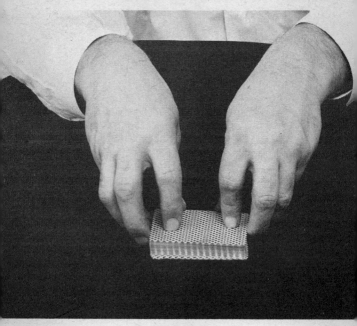

Fig. 6B. Shuffle

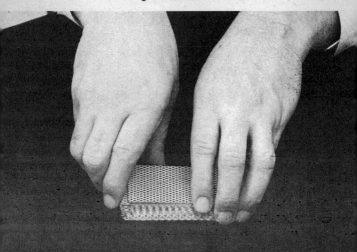

Fig. 7A. Shuffle

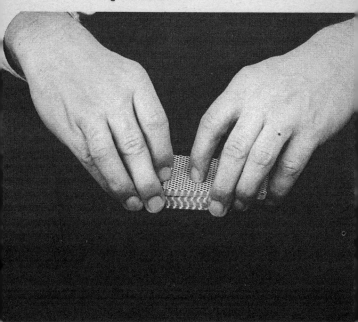

Fig. 7B. Shuffle

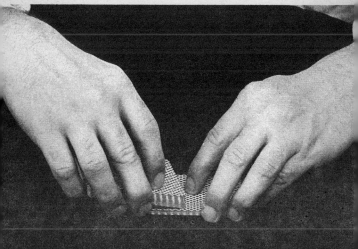

Fig. 7C. Shuffle

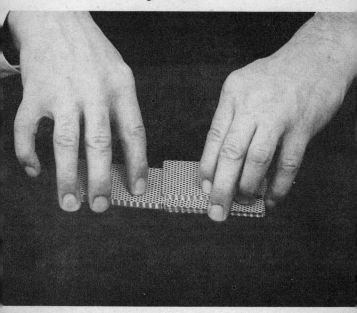

The illustrations for the seventh step (Figures 7A, 7B, and 7C) making a series of quick cuts. Most casino managers insist on these cuts because they are a protection against players following cards through the shuffle, and also because it adds showmanship to the procedure.

The cuts are made with the right hand removing the bottom three-fourths of the deck to the top, the middle finger of the left hand taking off a few of the cards, and the portion that is still in the right hand again being brought back to the top. This process is repeated so that the dealer has cut the deck three, four, or five times.

The movement of the cuts by the professional blackjack dealer is so fast that it is difficult actually to see the cards being taken off as his right hand moves out and in. The out and in movement is not straight out, but rather toward the upper right corner of the deck. This is important in order to keep the cards in the left hand from sliding out.

Burying the Top Card

After a player cuts the cards, the dealer picks the deck up with his right hand. As shown in Figure 8, the left thumb slides the top card to the left, down and under the deck. This move can be so fast that it is nearly impossible to see the card. Often players do not realize the dealer has buried a card.

Fig. 8. Bury

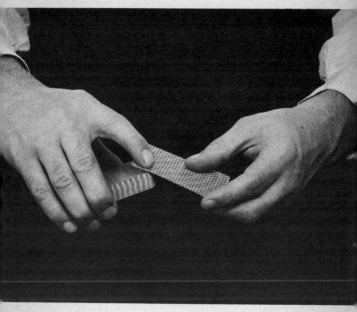

The Deal

Dealing the cards can cause many problems if the cards are not kicked out one at a time and in the correct spot. Figures 9A, 9B, and 9C show the grip. Fanning the deck is accomplished with the left thumb on the side of the deck. The illustrations also show the right thumb helping to fan the deck. The two-handed method is much easier and, for the beginner, the best method.

Figure 9C shows the left thumb in position for the deal. The left thumb pushes the top card to the right for the right thumb and index finger to grab. The grab is illustrated in Figure 10. The middle finger is in position to kick the card to the player. Figure 11 shows the fingers extended after the kick.

The dealer deals his up card by turning it up as if hitting a player (Figure 12). His down card is placed under the up card as in Figure 13. The dealer looks at his hole card when his up card is a 10 or an ace. The method most commonly used is seen in Figure 14.

Hitting, Collecting, and Paying

Blackjack is dealt from the dealer's left to his right. The players are also hit from left to right. After the dealer has finished all hitting, including his own, he pays or collects from his right to his left.

Figure 15 shows the method for holding the deck while hitting the player. This method keeps the cards from being seen by the player. Figures 16 and 17 illustrate the method for hitting a player. The middle finger is generally used to push the card lightly under the front edge of the wager.

Fig. 9A. Deal

Fig. 9B. Deal

Fig. 9C. Deal

Fig. 10. Deal

Fig. 11. Deal

Fig. 12. Deal

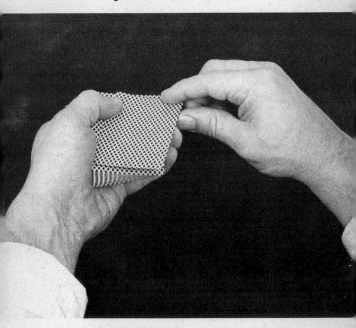

Fig. 13. Deal

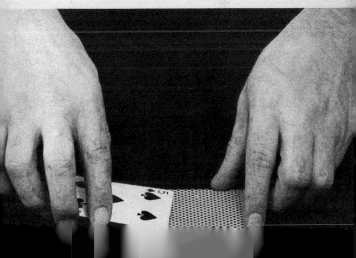

Fig. 14. Deal

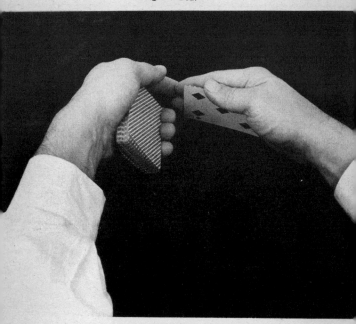

Fig. 15. Hitting

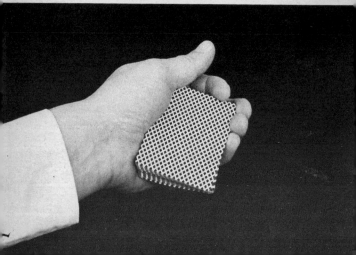

Fig. 16. Hitting

Fig. 17. Hitting

Figure 18 demonstrates the method used for holding the deck while turning the players' cards over or making a payoff with the left hand.

Figure 19 shows the way to pick up cards. When the dealer wants to make a payoff with the right hand, he transfers the picked up cards to the left hand. Care should be used to scoop up the cards in the sequence as picked up so that they can be given back to the players in sequence in case of a dispute over addition.

Fig. 18. Pick-up

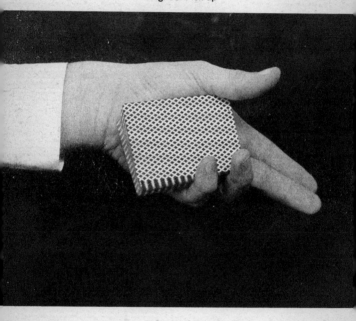

Fig. 19. Pick-up

18.

CASINOS, HONEST OR CROOKED?

ARE CASINOS honest or crooked? This is the most common question dealers are asked, and the answer is not easy. There are casinos all over the world and in every kind of environment. Besides, gambling is usually so emotional that almost any act, however innocent or valid, may be regarded with suspicion by a tense player.

The usual accusations leveled against dealers and pit bosses are these, listed in order of popularity:

1. A new dealer is sent into the game when a player is winning and thus something crooked must be in the works.

2. The dealer conceals the cards from the players.

3. The dealer makes mistakes that cause players to lose.

4. The dealer hits 20 and 21 far too often.

Let us briefly discuss each of these four charges.

A New Dealer Is Sent into the Game

When a player is winning, especially when he is betting heavily, he can usually be sure that a new dealer will be sent in. This is almost always viewed darkly by the winning player who suspects that the newcomer is a card sharp.

Sometimes there are good reasons for making a replacement; other times there aren't. The legitimate reasons are the most common. Dealers take a coffee break anywhere from six to ten times during an eight-hour stint; this means that a winning table is bound to have a new dealer at least once every hour. A more important reason for swtiching dealers—important, at any rate, from the point of view of the pit boss—is to send the best into a game where the bets are high. This is merely good business sense. In any endeavour the best people are given the most important assignments in order to hold costly mistakes down to a minimum.

A reason that makes no sense and yet harms nobody is based on pure superstition. Many pit bosses believe that changing the dealer will change bad luck to good at a winning table. Professional gamblers are inclined to be as illogical as amateur players.

Dealer Conceals Cards from Players

The fact that dealers hold the deck in the back of the hand and keep the cards from being seen is often taken as a sign that they must be cheating. Actually, dealers are taught to hold the deck in this way in order to thwart players who mark the cards. This is simply one of the methods by which casinos protect themselves from card cheats.

Dealer Makes Mistakes Which Cause Player to Lose

Dealing blackjack is an extremely demanding job. Dealing the cards, counting the totals, making the payoffs, talking with players, watching out for cheating is as fatiguing physically as it is mentally. Besides, most of the play is late at night when a person is not as alert as during the day. It is no wonder that dealers occasionally make mistakes.

At Harrah's Club in Reno and Lake Tahoe, the casino has a rule for nearly every kind of mistake. In other casinos, especially those on the Las Vegas Strip, dealers are expected to make few or no mistakes. At any rate, mistakes will happen, and they will cause a player to lose as often as they help him to win. Needless to say, a player will remember those mistakes which cost him money.

Dealer Hits 20 and 21 too Often

Players accuse dealers of cheating because the dealers hit

many more 20's and 21's than the players. Probably every black jack player has had this thought in back of his mind when th dealer is hitting well. There is always the old standby question Why can the dealer hit those stiffs while I'm hardly ever able to

The reason is both mechanical and psychological. Mechan cally, the dealer must hit all 12's, 13's, 14's, 15's, and 16' whereas the player hits about half of the stiffs. Consequently the player should only make about half as many. Psychologically players tend to forget about their winning hands while the often remember how a dealer won ten straight hands and ca describe every detail a year later.

Methods of Cheating

There are several ways that a dealer can cheat in blackjack all requiring a high degree of skill. The most common are called the *cold deck*, the *roll over*, and *seconds*.

The cold deck is the term used for stacking a deck and the dealing without a shuffle. This is the most difficult method o cheating because the dealer must be able to adjust the deck afte the cut.

More common and much easier than the cold deck is the rol over. Instead of completely stacking the deck and shuffling, the dealer will stack a couple of hands before collecting the cards o the next hand; he'll roll the deck in his hand so that the stacked portion is now on top. He then deals the stacked hands.

Seconds is the term used for dealing the second card from the top. This is not difficult, but the dealer must be able to peek ir order to take advantage of the seconds.

Ability to Cheat

Cheating while dealing isn't easy. Most dealers have their hands full trying to do a good job of dealing honestly.

I have dealt in six different casinos of various sizes, types and locations. Of all the dealers that I know, only two were capable of cheating, and of these two, one had a hard time finding work because the casino owners wouldn't trust him. The other dealer was a highly respected member of the State Athletic Commission, and was the type that would not cheat for any reason.

Casino owners know from long experience that dealers who would cheat for the house would just as soon cheat against it.

It is far easier, and more profitable, for a crooked dealer to have a friend play at the dealer's table and deal the friend winning hands. Nearly all casinos have had this trouble at one time or another.

Fig. 20. Peeking

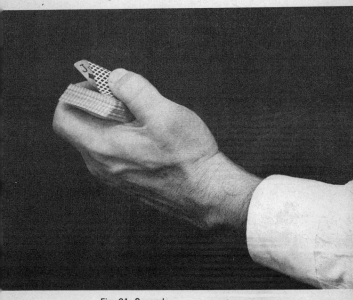

Fig. 21. Seconds

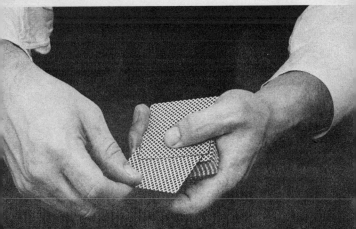

19.

CASINOS

IT IS THE PURPOSE of this chapter to survey some of the foremost casinos in the United States and throughout the western world. The size is presented according to the amount of gambling equipment, not by the dollar volume or the dimensions of the building. All information relating to Nevada casinos was acquired by personal visits.

LAS VEGAS, NEVADA (STRIP)

The Strip is generally regarded as the most fabulous place in the world for gambling and entertainment. Unlike most gambling spots in Nevada, vacationers often spend one or two weeks there. The excellent golfing, swimming, fine restaurants, and the large quantity of top entertainment give the vacationers plenty to do besides gambling.

The gambling limits for blackjack are $1 minimum to $500 maximum at nearly all Strip hotels. These rules have been standard for years, with the exception of one short period when management was frightened into tightening them. A decrease in play and profits resulted in restoring the former rules. Casinos on the Strip generally require the dealer to stand on soft 17. The player may take insurance and he may double on any two cards.

As a rule, the gamblers on the strip are wealthier and make larger wagers than at other Nevada gambling centers. While dealing at the Stardust Hotel, I often dealt to players that were betting the limits. During an exceptionally busy weekend, it was common to see $25 minimum tables, where the lowest wager for the six players was over $250. In Reno and Lake Tahoe, this sort of gambling is extremely rare.

The future for the Strip seems to be brighter each year. Management has improved, and the hotels are increasing their size at a fast pace to keep up with the growth of the community.

ALADDIN HOTEL. Games include sixteen blackjack tables, six crap tables, two roulette wheels, Keno, and approximately four hundred slot machines.

Entertainment consists of name performers or burlesque in the show room and lounge. Good hotel rates.

BONANZA (hotel-casino). Fourteen blackjack tables, dealer stands on soft 17; player may double on any two cards; insurance is allowed. Other games include four crap tables, two roulette wheels, 300 slots, Keno, and Big 6.

Entertainment in showroom and lounge.

CAESAR'S PALACE (hotel-casino). Games include nineteen blackjack tables, eight crap tables, three roulette wheels, Baccarat, and approximately two hundred slot machines.

Entertainment is of the big name, production type. The main showroom seats eight hundred people, and the main convention hall seats two thousand. There are a number of other reception rooms as well as lavish outdoor areas for dining and meetings.

CASTAWAYS (hotel-casino). Approximately nine blackjack, one crap, and one roulette tables. Dealer stands on soft 17; player may double on any two cards; insurance is allowed. A Howard Hughes casino.

CIRCUS CIRCUS CASINO. This very unusual casino has a flying trapeze act, doing its act directly over the blackjack tables. In addition, they shoot human cannon balls over the tables. Completely circling the casino are a variety of carnival booths for throwing balls and the works. Casino games include fifteen blackjack tables, four crap tables, one roulette, Keno, Big 6, and 500 slots. In addition to the circus acts, they have a small show-room and a lounge.

DESERT INN HOTEL. There are eleven blackjack tables. Dealer stands on soft 17; player may double on any two cards; insurance is allowed. Other games include seven crap tables, two roulette wheels, and approximately 210 slot machines. All blackjack tables use the shoe with four decks of cards.

Entertainment is excellent, with name performers in the show room, various acts in the lounge, and dancing in the Sky Room. The Desert Inn has its own golf course.

DUNES HOTEL. Nineteen blackjack tables. Dealer stands on soft 17; player may double on any two cards; insurance is al-lowed. Other games include eight crap tables, two roulette wheels, one Baccarat, poker, and approximately 230 slot ma-chines.

Entertainment in the show room usually consists of produc-tion shows, with a large cast of show girls and dancers. The Persian Room Lounge has had excellent lounge acts in the past. The new Top of the Strip room has a name orchestra for danc-ing. The Dunes has its own golf course. Howard Hughes owned.

FLAMINGO HOTEL. Fourteen blackjack tables. Dealer stands on soft 17; player may double on any two cards. Other games include six crap tables, two roulette wheels, three hundred fifty slot machines, Keno, and Baccarat. No shoes.

Entertainment in the show room presents name performers backed by dancing line. The lounge is known for bands such as Harry James and Count Basie.

FRONTIER HOTEL. Games include sixteen blackjack tables, seven crap tables, two roulette wheels, Keno, Baccarat, and 300 slot machines. All blackjack games use the four deck shoe.

Name entertainment in the showroom and lounge. Owned by Howard Hughes.

HACIENDA HOTEL. Fifteen blackjack tables. Dealer must hit soft 17; player may double on any two cards; insurance is allowed. Two or three games use the shoe. Other games include four crap tables, two roulette wheels, one Big Six Wheel, Keno, poker, Pan, and approximately 150 slot machines.

Comedy entertainment in the showroom. There is dancing in the lounge.

The Riviera Hotel exemplifies the Las Vegas Strip luxury hotel-casinos

INTERNATIONAL HOTEL. The new king of casinos has thirty blackjack tables, nine crap tables, three roulette wheels, two Baccarat, Keno, Big Six, and 850 slots. Blackjack rules allow doubling on any two cards; dealer stands on soft 17. The four deck shoes are used on many of the tables.

Entertainment in the showroom has top stars, such as Barbra Streisand and Elvis Presley.

LANDMARK HOTEL. Twelve blackjack tables. Dealer stands on soft 17; player may double on any two cards; insurance is allowed. Other games include five crap tables, one roulette, Keno, and 170 slots. Big name entertainment. Howard Hughes owned.

RIVIERA HOTEL. Seventeen blackjack tables. Dealer must stand on soft 17; player may double on any two cards; insurance is allowed. Other games include six crap tables, two roulette wheels, Big Six, approximately 400 slot machines, and Baccarat. No shoes for blackjack.

Entertainment in the show room is usually a Broadway play or a name performer. The lounge offers comedy acts and occasional jazz bands. Dean Martin owns interest.

Downtown Las Vegas

SAHARA HOTEL. Twenty blackjack tables. Dealer must stand on soft 17; player may double on any two cards; insurance is allowed. Other games include eight crap tables, three roulette wheels, Keno, poker, and approximately 600 slot machines.

Entertainment includes name entertainers in the show room and a popular lounge which goes heavy on comedy. Del Webb owned.

SANDS HOTEL. Fourteen blackjack tables. The dealer must stand on soft 17; player may double on any two cards; insurance is allowed; games are dealt out of a shoe. Other games include six crap tables, one double layout roulette, Baccarat, and 300 slot machines.

Entertainment in the show room is always good. The lounge usually presents musical entertainment. Howard Hughes owned.

SILVER SLIPPER (casino only). Ten blackjack tables, all using the shoe. Dealer must stand on soft 17; player may double on any two cards; insurance is allowed. Other games include two crap tables, one roulette wheel, Keno, and 120 slot machines.

Entertainment in the show room is the adult kind. A Howard Hughes owned casino.

STARDUST HOTEL. Twenty-five blackjack tables. Dealer must stand on soft 17; player may double on any two cards; insurance is allowed. Other games include six crap tables, three roulette, one Big Six, Keno, poker, Pan, and approximately 700 slot machines.

Entertainment in the show room is the *Lido de Paris* show. The Lido show is the essential show for most Las Vegas vacationers. Each year the settings and part of the cast are changed. The lounge show has a revolving stage for continuous entertainment. Acts in the lounge are usually comedy or singing or dancing groups.

THUNDERBIRD HOTEL. Thirteen blackjack tables. Dealer must stand on soft 17; the player may double on any two cards; insurance is allowed. Other games include two crap tables, one roulette, one Big Six, and 250 slot machines.

Showroom and lounge entertainment. Del Webb owned.

HOTEL TROPICANA. Fourteen blackjack tables, all using the shoe. Dealer must stand on soft 17; player may double on any two cards; insurance is allowed. Other games include six crap tables, two roulette wheels, and approximately 270 slot machines.

Entertainment in the show room is the Folies Bergere. The Folies Bergere is similar to the *Lido,* with gorgeous sets, show girls and dancing. The lounge has high quality name entertainment. The hotel has its own golf course.

LAS VEGAS, NEVADA (DOWNTOWN)

Downtown Las Vegas is similar to Reno, Nevada, in size and type of operation. The big business in both of these downtown gambling areas is the slot machine. Keno, blackjack, and craps have heavy play, but the income is often lower than from slot machines.

CLUB BINGO. This club has approximately 120 slot machines and Bingo.

CAROUSEL (casino only). Seven blackjack tables. Dealer must hit on soft 17; player may double on any two cards; insurance is allowed. Other games include two crap tables, one roulette wheel, Keno, and approximately 190 slot machines.

No entertainment.

EL CORTEZ HOTEL. Eight blackjack tables. The dealer must hit on soft 17; player may double on any two cards; insurance is allowed. Other games include three crap tables, one roulette, and approximately 230 slot machines.

Three or four small groups entertain in the bar.

HOTEL FREMONT. Eighteen blackjack tables. Dealer must hit on soft 17; player may double on any two cards; insurance is allowed. Other games include five crap tables, three roulette wheels, Keno, Pan, poker, and approximately six hundred slot machines.

Entertainment is usually excellent in the Fiesta Room, backed by one of the best show bands in Las Vegas. Dancing in the sky room and a lounge show rounds out the entertainment. The Fremont Hotel has the distinction of being the world's tallest resort hotel, thirty-two stories high.

GOLDEN GATE (hotel-casino). Eight blackjack tables. Dealer must hit on soft 17; player may double on any two cards; insurance is allowed. Other games include three crap tables, one roulette wheel, Keno, and approximately 275 slot machines.

No entertainment.

GOLDEN NUGGET (casino only). Twenty-six blackjack tables. Dealer must hit on soft 17; player may double on any two cards; insurance is allowed. Other games include seven crap tables, four roulette wheels, poker, and 650 slot machines.

There is entertainment in the lounge.

HORSESHOE (casino only). Over twenty blackjack tables. Dealer must hit on soft 17; player may double on any two cards; insurance is allowed. Other games include four crap tables, two roulette wheels, one Big Six wheel, Keno, and approximately 330 slot machines.

No entertainment.

LAS VEGAS CLUB (casino only). Five blackjack tables. Dealer must hit soft 17; player may double on any two cards; insurance is allowed. Other games include two crap tables, one roulette wheel, Keno, poker, Pan, and approximately 200 slot machines.

No entertainment.

MINT HOTEL-CASINO. Twenty-four blackjack tables. Dealer must hit on soft 17; player may double on any two cards; insurance is allowed. Other games include six crap tables, three roulette wheels, two Big Six wheels, Keno, approximately 850 slot machines, Baccarat, and Faro.

Entertainment in the Merri-Mint Theatre. There is dancing at the top of the Mint. Del Webb owned.

PIONEER CLUB (casino only). Has 160 slots.

FOUR QUEENS HOTEL-CASINO. Eighteen blackjack tables, four crap tables, one roulette wheel, Keno, and approximately four hundred slot machines. Entertainment is provided in the lounge.

SHOWBOAT HOTEL-CASINO. The address is 2800 Fremont Street, not in the downtown area.

Nine blackjack tables, two crap tables, one roulette wheel, bingo, and 340 slot machines

Entertainment includes lounge acts in the bar and a bowling alley. This casino is frequented primarily by the family residents of Las Vegas and the families staying at the hotel.

LAKE TAHOE, SOUTH SHORE (STATELINE, NEVADA)

Lake Tahoe is over 6,000 feet high in the Sierra Mountains. The lake is divided down the center, with the east side in the state of Nevada and the west side in the state of California. The gambling areas are on the borders on both ends of the lake.

The South Shore is the most popular end of the lake, with three large gambling casinos concentrated within a few hundred feet of each other. The gambling industry is in Nevada, but most of the motels and employee homes are in California.

The ski season in the winter and water sports in the summer are big attractions for the casinos. Golfing is good.

Women blackjack dealers by far outnumber men in Lake Tahoe.

BARNEY'S (casino only). Seven blackjack tables. Dealer must hit on soft 17; player may double on 9, 10, or 11; insurance is not allowed.

Barney's has one crap table, one roulette wheel, Keno, poker, and approximately 330 slot machines.

HARRAH'S CLUB. There are approximately forty-five black-jack tables. Dealer must hit on soft 17; player may double on 10 or 11; insurance is permitted. Several double deck games are played. Besides the blackjack tables, Harrah's has ten crap tables, four roulette wheels, approximately 1,300 slot machines, two separate Keno games, bingo, and a race book. There are several types of slots, including jumbo dollar machines.

The South Shore Room has big name attractions with a name band and a cast of showgirls and dancers. The Stateline Lounge has four or five performing acts that rotate from evening to early morning. Lounge entertainment generally includes a big name jazz band, a popular singer and various comedy and dancing groups. Harrah's Club provides a recreation center with ping pong, television, movies, and miscellaneous games. A nursery is included.

HARVEY'S WAGON WHEEL (hotel-casino). Approximately forty-six blackjack tables. Dealer must hit soft 17; player may double on 10 or 11; insurance is allowed. Other games at Harvey's include eleven crap tables, five roulette wheels, three Big Six wheels, Keno, bingo, and approximately 1,400 slot machines. The slots include dollar machines, green back machines, and electric blackjack machines.

A show room, two lounge show areas, and dancing at the "top of the wheel" provide the entertainment. The acts are mostly name groups, heavy on the comedy. Convention facilities for groups of a thousand or less.

SAHARA TAHOE HOTEL. Forty-seven blackjack tables. Dealer must hit soft 17; player may double down on 10 or 11; insurance is allowed. Other games include eight crap tables, four roulette wheels, Big Six, Keno, and approximately a thousand slot machines.

The casino is the longest in the world, 110 yards long and 63 yards wide. The hotel is fourteen stories high, has 350 rooms. The High Sierra Room is one of the finest theatre restaurants in the world, with a capacity of approximately eight hundred for the dinner shows, and twelve hundred for cocktail shows. The huge stage is hydraulic operated and includes miles of overhead wiring and automatic set equipment. Entertainment is generally big name stars. The Aspen Grove Theatre and the Juniper showbar both have no minimum or cover charge with top lounge acts. In addition to the show rooms, there is a huge ballroom that will accommodate conventions of a thousand people.

SOUTH TAHOE NUGGET (casino only). Five blackjack tables. Dealer hits soft 17; player may double on 10 or 11; insurance is allowed. Other games are one crap table, Keno, and approximately 200 slot machines.

LAKE TAHOE, NORTH SHORE (CRYSTAL BAY, NEVADA)

The North Shore of Lake Tahoe caters to the summer vacationers and fewer over-nighters than the South Shore. With less entertainment provided, the North Shore casinos have had an uphill struggle to compete with the larger South Shore casinos. The rules for blackjack have changed frequently at the North Shore and may change again.

CAL NEVA (hotel-casino). Approximately eleven blackjack tables. Dealer must hit soft 17; player may double on 10 or 11 with two cards only; insurance is allowed. Other equipment normally includes two crap tables, a roulette wheel, and approximately 275 slots.

Entertainment has been excellent in past years, with the top names in show business performing in the show room. The casino-hotel has had a rocky road throughout the years, with frequent change in ownership.

CRYSTAL BAY CLUB (casino only). Seven blackjack tables. Dealer must hit soft 17; player may double on 10 or 11; insurance is allowed. Other games include one crap table, one roulette wheel, Keno, and approximately 350 slot machines.

Entertainment is limited to dancing and a lounge.

KING'S CASTLE. The newest and most plush hotel on the North Shore of Lake Tahoe. Buddy Hackett is part owner. The casino has fifteen blackjack tables with Las Vegas rules; player may double on any two cards; insurance is allowed; the shoe is used on eleven of the tables. Other games include five crap tables, one roulette, Keno, Baccarat, and 235 slots.

Name entertainment.

NEVADA LODGE. Ten blackjack tables. Dealer must hit soft 17; player may double on any two cards; insurance is allowed.

Other games include three crap tables, one double layout roulette, Keno, and approximately six hundred slot machines.

Entertainment in the Topaz Room varies from production shows to trios.

NORTH SHORE CLUB HOTEL. Ten blackjack tables. Dealer must hit soft 17; player may double on any two cards; insurance is allowed. Other equipment includes two crap tables, two roulette wheels, and 110 slot machines.

Entertainment is usually good with small acts.

TAHOE NUGGET (casino only, closed in winter). One blackjack table. Dealer hits soft 17; player may double on any two cards. Other equipment includes 75 slot machines and electric blackjack.

RENO, NEVADA

Reno is northern Nevada's largest city, and like Lake Tahoe, it draws customers primarily from northern California. Although Reno has been known for its slot machines, Harolds Club with sixty blackjack tables and Harrah's with fifty are leaders in blackjack capacity. Entertainment in Reno is fair, but cannot be compared with Las Vegas.

CAL NEVA (casino only). Ten blackjack tables. Dealer must hit soft 17; player may double on 10 or 11; insurance is allowed. Other games include two crap tables, two roulette wheels, Keno, and 450 slot machines.

No entertainment.

HAROLDS CLUB (casino only). Approximately sixty blackjack tables. Dealers must hit soft 17; player may double on any two cards totaling less than 11. Other games include approximately seven crap tables, one chuck-a-luck, four roulette wheels, Keno, Pan, and approximately seven hundred slot machines.

Entertainment is provided in the lounge and two small show rooms. Occasional name entertainment, but mostly small groups. Howard Hughes owned.

HARRAH'S CLUB RENO. Fifty blackjack tables. Dealer must hit soft 17; player may double on 10 or 11; insurance is allowed. Other games include eight crap tables, four roulette wheels, bingo, Keno, and approximately one thousand two hundred slot machines, including the giant "Buck Machines."

Entertainment is in the lounge with several name groups appearing per evening.

Harrah's automobile collection, which is on display, is the largest in the world with more than nine hundred autos.

HOLIDAY HOTEL. Eleven blackjack tables. Dealer must hit soft 17; player may double on 10 or 11; no insurance is allowed. Other games include one crap table, one roulette wheel, and 200 slot machines.

Entertainment in the lounge.

HORSESHOE CLUB (casino only). Eleven blackjack tables. Dealer must hit soft 17; player may double on 10 or 11; insurance is allowed. Other games include two crap tables, one roulette wheel, Keno, and 250 slot machines.

No entertainment.

MAPES HOTEL. Seven blackjack tables. Dealer must hit soft 17; player may double on 10 or 11. Other games include one crap table, one roulette wheel, and 200 slot machines.

Entertainment is in the show room and is usually good.

MONEY TREE CASINO. Four blackjack tables; dealer must hit soft 17; player may double on 10 or 11; insurance is allowed. Other games include one crap table, one roulette, 190 slots, and Keno.

NEVADA CLUB (casino only). Twelve blackjack tables. Dealer must hit soft 17; player may double on 10 or 11; insurance is allowed. Other games include six crap tables, one double layout roulette table, Keno, eight hundred slot machines, and one chuck-a-luck.

NUGGET CASINO. One blackjack table, 190 slots.

OVERLAND CASINO. Four blackjack tables, one crap table, one roulette wheel, 180 slots, and Keno.

PALACE CLUB (casino only). Six blackjack tables. Dealer must hit soft 17; player may double on 10 or 11; no insurance. Other games include one crap table, one roulette, Keno, and 200 slot machines.

PRIMA DONNA (casino only). Fifteen blackjack tables. Dealer must hit soft 17; player may double on 10 or 11; no insurance. Other games include two crap tables, one roulette wheel, Keno, and over 500 slot machines.

The theatre restaurant generally has entertainment.

SILVER SPUR CASINO. One blackjack table, one crap table, one roulette, and 170 slot machines. No entertainment.

EAST RENO, (SPARKS, NEVADA)

NUGGET (casino and hotel). Nineteen blackjack tables. Dealer must hit soft 17; player may double on 10 or 11; no insurance. Other games include two crap tables, two roulette wheels, one Big Six wheel, Keno, bingo, and approximately six hundred slot machines, including four electric 21's, and Big Bertha and paper dollar machines.

Entertainment in the 750 seat Circus Room theatre restaurant includes big name performers with production numbers. The hotel rates are among the lowest in Nevada.

CARSON CITY, NEVADA

CARSON CITY NUGGET (casino only). Nine blackjack tables. Dealer must hit soft 17; player may double on 10 or 11 with two cards only; no insurance. One dollar to $100 limits. Other games include one crap table, one roulette wheel, Keno, bingo and approximately 310 slot machines.

Entertainment in the lounge is weak.

The Nugget is Carson City's major casino. Two small casinos operate with one or two blackjack tables and less than 100 slots combined.

CASINOS AROUND THE WORLD

CARIBBEAN

Blackjack, craps, and roulette are the three most popular games in Caribbean casinos. Slot machines and various casino side games are not often found in the quiet Caribbean casinos.

Puerto Rico has more casinos than any other Caribbean country. San Juan has four casinos: the Caribe Hilton, San Juan Intercontinental, La Concha, and the Flambuoyan. Santurce has the Condado Beach Hotel. Ponce has the Ponce Intercontinental. Aquadilla has the Montemar Hotel. All these Puerto Rico casinos are rigidly controlled by the government.

A typical Puerto Rico Hotel casino is the Condado Beach Hotel in Santurce. It has four blackjack tables, one crap table, and two roulette wheels. The rules for blackjack require the dealer to stand on all 17's, and the player may double on 11 only. Blackjack table limits are $1 to $50. The men are required to wear a jacket and a tie. The entertainment is American-native.

Other casinos in the Caribbean include the Curacao Intercontinental Hotel, Netherlands Antilles; El Panama Hilton Hotel Casino, Panama City, Panama; Embajador Hotel, Dominican Republic; Aruba, Netherlands Antilles; International Casino, Haiti; Bahamian Club, Nassau (Bahamas). The Bahamian Club is the casino referred to in *Thunderball*, the Ian Fleming novel and movie.

BELGIUM

Belgium has casinos in Blankenberghe, Chaud Fontaine, Dinant, Knokke-Le Zoute, Middlekerke, Namur, Ostend, and Spa. Most of these casinos stay open throughout the year. The games played in these casinos are roulette, baccara, and chemin de fer. The Casino-Kursaal in Ostend is the major casino, although others are quite large. The Casino of Spa has twelve roulette tables, two baccara, and one chemin de fer. The casino of Dinant has seven roulette wheels and two baccara-chemin de fer.

CASINO-KURSAAL D'OSTENDE. Europe's largest and most modern casino is the Casino-Kursaal. It has fifteen roulette wheels with double layouts, and fourteen baccara tables. Although this doesn't seem large in comparison with the Lake

Tahoe, Nevada, casinos, each table can seat many more players than the typical American roulette and blackjack games. The roulette betting limits are the equivalent to American limits.

Roulette throughout Belgium is played with 36 numbers and without any zeros. The profit of the casino comes from a 5 percent charge deducted from all winning bets. This is equivalent to a 2½ percent house advantage, compared to a 5¼ percent house advantage for the American roulette layout. Baccara is played at similar odds as roulette since 5 percent is from the winning bets. The house advantage for the Belgium Baccara is slightly higher than the Las Vegas style Baccarat-Chemin de Fer game.

The Casino-Kursaal, which is a short distance by air from London and Paris, has similar convention facilities to those of Caesar's Palace, the new Las Vegas casino. The hotel accommodations at Ostend, however, are separate from the Casino-Kursaal, whereas the Las Vegas casinos are also hotels. The entertainment in the Grand Concert Hall presents concerts and ballets. There are two separate cabaret night clubs for dancing and entertainment. Numerous large balls are held throughout the year, the largest being the Dead Rat Ball with eight orchestras playing to eight thousand people. The resort area features golfing and horse racing as well as swimming and other typical resort sports.

Kursaal d'Ostende in Belgium

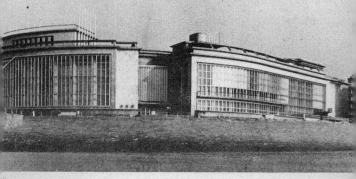

FRENCH RIVIERA

The Riviera is perhaps best known for the famous casino of
Monte Carlo. Besides this famous casino, there are casinos in
Cannes, Juan-Les-Pins, Deauville, La Baule, Touquet, and
Evian.

CASINO DE MONTE CARLO (Monaco). Monte Carlo has
twelve roulette wheels, four baccara, one chemin de fer, one
crap table, one trente et quarante, six boule, and slot machines.
Limits for craps is the equivalent to one dollar minimum and
$250 maximum. Limits for roulette is equivalent to one dollar
to $2,500.

Entertainment at Monte Carlo includes concerts, operas, plays,
movies, and most water and snow sports.

CASINO MUNICIPAL DE CANNES (Cannes, France). The
Casino Municipal De Cannes is typical of the French Riviera
casinos. They have four roulette wheels and six baccara layouts.
The baccara games have no limits and the roulette wheels have
the equivalent of a $2,000 limit. Roulette is played with one
zero as in Monte Carlo.

This casino is one of a large chain which owns the casinos
in Deauville, La Baule, Le Touquet, and Juan-Les-Pins. The
Casino de Cannes is open from November 1st until May 31st.
Entertainment includes a theatre and a cabaret night club. Men
must wear ties and jackets.

ITALY

The Casino Municipale in San Remo, Italy, is one of Europe's largest. There are sixteen roulette wheels, nine chemin de
fer-baccara games, and four trente et quarante games. The limits
on roulette are approximately one dollar to $2,500.00, and on
trente et quarante approximately $3 to $450. The roulette wheels
have one zero and rules are similar to Monto Carlo. The casino
is open all year round and its entertainment includes operas,
comedies, musical plays, and floor shows. The casinos in Cam-
pione, Venice, and St. Vincent are of less importance.

GERMANY

Casinos and gambling halls are common in Germany. The
gambling halls or *Spielhallen* are primarily slot machine casinos.
The main game in the regular casino is roulette.

The Kurhaus in Baden Baden and the casinos in Lindau and Constance are the best known of the German casinos. Typical of German casinos is the Internationale Spielbank in Lindau/ Bodensee Germany. The casino has eight roulette wheels and one chemin de fer-baccara. Limits are approximately 50 cents to $600 for roulette, and $2.50 to $1,500 for baccara.

ENGLAND

The English casinos are now among the best known in the world because of the Ian Fleming novels. Crockfords, Quents, and the Metropole are the major card clubs in England. English casinos, unlike most others, require a player to be a member of the club or a guest of a member. Chemin-de-fer and roulette are the main games. Casinos in England are not allowed to have a casino edge, but the private clubs get around the law through various means.

CASINOS ELSEWHERE

Other countries to have legal gambling casinos include Austria, Cambodia, Chile, Ghana, Macau, Portugal, and Swaziland. In nearly all of these countries, the major games are roulette, baccara or chemin de fer.

Swaziland is the latest country to have legalized casino gambling. The new casino-hotel, called Swaziland Spa, opened in 1966. Swaziland is one of the British territories in South Africa. The casino has four blackjack tables. Dealer must hit soft 17; player may double on 9, 10, or 11; no insurance is allowed. Other equipment includes five roulette wheels with one zero, five chemin-de-fer tables, and twelve slot machines. Entertainment includes production shows, dancing, golf course, tennis, riding, bowls, and swimming. The casino flies customers from Johannesburg, South Africa, and from Lourenco Marques, Portuguese Mozambique.

SELF-TEST

1. The third baseman should not hit a stiff if the dealer has a 3 showing because he might take away the dealer's break card. **T F**

2. Never take insurance unless you have a good hand. **T F**

3. It is to your advantage for the deck to be heavy in 10's. **T F**

4. If you have a 14 and the dealer has a 2 up, what action should you take if the case is even? . . . . . .

5. If you have a 10 and the dealer has a 10 up, what action should you take if the case is even? . . . . . .

6. You have two 5's. If the dealer has a 9 up, what action should you take if the case is even? . . . . . .

7. If you have two 9's and the dealer has a 7 up, what action should you take if the case is even? . . . . . .

8. If you have 9 and the dealer has a 7 up, what action should you take if the case is even? . . . . . .

9. If you have a soft 17 and the dealer has a 4 up, what action should you take if the case is even? . . . . . .

10. If you have two aces and the dealer has a 10 up, what action should you take if the case is even? . . . . . .

11. If you have a soft 13 and the dealer has a 9 up, what action should the player take if the case is even? . . . . . .

12. If you have a soft 18 and the dealer has a 9 up, what action should you take if the case is even? . . . . . .

13. When casing the deck, the multiplier, when half the cards have been seen, is one. **T F**

14. When one-fourth of the deck has been cased, what is the multiplier? . . . . . .

15. When all but twelve cards have been cased, multiply the case by . . . . . .

16. Insurance should be taken if there is a minus in 10's.   T F

17. When you have a 14 and the dealer has a 2, 3, or 4 up, what overbalance of 10's will change the action from stand to hit?   . . . . . .

18. If you have 14 and the dealer has a 9 up, will a case of two plus in 10's change the action from hit to stand?   . . . . . .

19. If you have 14 and the dealer has a 6 up, will a case of three minus in 10's change the action from stand to hit?   . . . . . .

20. If the player has 11 and the dealer has a 9 up, will a one minus in 10's change the action to hit?   . . . . . .

21. If the player has a soft 18 and the dealer has a 4 up, will a one minus in 10's indicate a double situation?   . . . . . .

22. If you have 9 and the dealer has a 7 up, what is the overbalance of 10's needed to double?   . . . . . .

23. If you have 8 and the dealer has a 6 up with a case of one plus in 10's, what is the action?   . . . . . .

24. If you have two aces and the dealer has an 8 up, what case in 10's will change the action from split to hit?   . . . . . .

25. If you have two 9's and the dealer has a 3 up, what action should the player take if the case is one minus in 10's?   . . . . . .

26. If you have two 3's and the dealer's up is 8, what case is needed in 10's to split?   . . . . . .

27. If you have two 5's, what case is needed to split the pair?   . . . . . .

28. If you have two 8's and the dealer has an ace showing, what case is needed in 10's to hit?   . . . . . .

29. If you have two 2's and the dealer has a 3 up, what action in 10's is needed to change the action from split to hit?   . . . . . .

30. If you have two 9's and the dealer has a 7 up, will a case of two plus in 10's show a split action? ......

31. For advanced casing, if the dealer deals two cards to each player and then reshuffles, what is the case if it was three aces, one plus in 10's, and one plus in small cards before shuffling? ......

32. What is the case for medium cards in question 31 before reshuffling? ......

33. If you have 12 and the dealer has a 2 up, what action should the player take if the case is two aces, one plus in 10's, and one plus in small cards? ......

34. If you have 12 or 13, what cards will have the most effect on the action? ......

35. If you have 15 and the dealer has a 10 up, what action is needed in small cards to have a stand action? ......

36. If you have 15 and the dealer has a 5 up, what should the action be if the case is two aces, even 10's and two plus in small cards? ....

37. If you have 12 and the dealer has an ace up, what action should be taken if the case is two plus in 10's and two plus in small cards? ......

38. If you have 14 and the dealer has a 3 up, what case is needed to change the action in advanced variations? ......

39. If the case is two aces, one plus in 10's, and one minus in small cards, with three-fourths of the deck having been cased, what is the case as concerns the tables? ......

40. If you have a soft 17 and the dealer has a 5, what action should you take if the case is two aces, one minus in 10's, and one minus in small cards? ......

41. If you have two 6's and the dealer has a 3 up card, what action should you take if the case is two aces, two plus in 10's, and one minus in small cards? ......

42. If you have two 8's, and the dealer has a 10 up card, what action should you take if the count is one ace, one minus in 10's, and two plus in small cards?   . . . . . .

43. If you have 10 and the dealer has a 3 up card, what action should you take if the count is three aces, two minus in 10's, and one plus in small cards?   . . . . . .

44. If you have 11 and the dealer has an 8 up card, what action should you take if the count is three aces, one minus in 10's, even in small cards, if ten cards are still uncased?   . . . . . .

45. If you have 16 and the dealer has an ace up card, what action should you take if the count is two aces, one plus in 10's, two minus in small cards, with two-thirds of the deck uncased?   . . . . . .

46. If you have 12 and the dealer has a 5 up card, what action should you take if the count is four aces, one minus in 10's, one minus in small cards with three-fourths of the deck cased?   . . . . . .

47. If you have two 2's, and the dealer has a 5, what action should you take if the count is two aces, one minus in 10's, and four minus in small cards with two-thirds of the deck cased?   . . . . . .

48. If you have a soft 15 and the dealer has a 6 showing, what should be the action taken if doubling on any two cards is allowed, and the count is two aces, two minus in 10's, and one plus in small cards?   . . . . . .

49. If you have 10 and the dealer has a 9 up card, what should be the action if the count is one ace, two minus in 10's, one plus in small cards, and one-third of the deck has been cased?   . . . . . .

50. If you have a 12 and the dealer has a 7, what action should you take if the count is two aces, two plus in 10's, and two minus in small cards?   . . . . . .

ANSWERS TO THE TEST

1. False
2. False
3. True
4. Stand
5. Double
6. Double
7. Stand
8. Hit
9. Double; if doubling not allowed, then hit.
10. Split
11. Hit
12. Hit
13. True
14. ⅔
15. 2
16. False
17. 2—
18. No

19. Yes
20. Yes
21. Yes
22. 1+
23. Double
24. 3—
25. Stand
26. 1—
27. Never split 5's (double or hit)
28. 1—
29. 2—
30. Yes
31. 1 ace, 1—, 1—
32. 2—
33. Stand
34. Medium Cards

35. 1—S
36. Stand
37. Stand
38. 2—T
39. 2 aces, 2+, 2—
40. Hit
41. Hit
42. Hit
43. Double
44. Hit
45. Stand
46. Hit
47. Split
48. Hit
49. Double
50. Hit

Grade 2 points for each question.

          92-100 = A
          84-92 = B
          76-84 = C
          66-76 = D
          Below 66 = F